THE SUPREME COURT DECISIONS ON THE CANADIAN CONSTITUTION

THE SUPREME COURT DECISIONS ON THE CANADIAN CONSTITUTION

James Lorimer & Company, Publishers
Toronto, 1981

ISBN 0-88862-539-1 cloth
ISBN 0-88862-538-3 paper

Cover design: Don Fernley

Canadian Cataloguing in Publication Data

Main entry under title:
The Supreme Court decisions on the Canadian
constitution

ISBN 0-88862-539-1 (cloth)   ISBN 0-88862-538-3
(paper)

1. Canada — Constitutional law — Cases. 2. Canada
— Constitutional law — Amendments. I. Canada.
Supreme Court.

KE4216.35.C6S96   342.71'032'02643   C81-095147-9

James Lorimer & Company, Publishers
Egerton Ryerson Memorial Building
35 Britain Street
Toronto
M5A 1R7

Printed and bound in Canada

6 5 4 3 2 1   81 82 83 84 85 86

ACKNOWLEDGEMENTS

We would like to acknowledge the assistance and cooperation of The Halifax Chronicle-Herald in making available the typesetting of the court decisions.

J.L.

CONTENTS

Introduction   by James Lorimer   *page vii*

The Questions   *page xvii*

The Action, the Parties and Counsel   *page xix*

1   **Legality: The Majority Decision**
    by Chief Justice Laskin and Judges Dickson,
    Beetz, Estey, McIntyre, Chouinard and
    Lamer   *page 1*

2   **Legality: The Minority Decision**
    by Judges Martland and Ritchie   *page 46*

3   **Constitutional Convention: The Majority
    Decision**
    by Judges Martland, Ritchie, Dickson, Beetz,
    Chouinard and Lamer   *page 82*

4   **Constitutional Convention: The Minority
    Decision**
    by Chief Justice Laskin and Judges Estey and
    McIntyre   *page 117*

INTRODUCTION TO THIS EDITION

JAMES LORIMER

In September 1981, the Supreme Court of Canada delivered its decisions on a set of constitutional questions posed to it in May 1981 by the federal and provincial governments. The questions arose out of the plan by the federal government, led by Pierre Elliott Trudeau, to patriate the British North America Act — after having the British Parliament add to it an amending formula — and entrench in it a Canadian Charter of Rights and Freedoms. The federal government's action was to be in the form of a joint resolution approved by the House of Commons and the Senate, requesting these actions from Britain. Once this request was sent to London and acted on by the British Parliament, the last vestiges of the colonial relationship between Canada and Britain would be ended. Canada would have its own constitution, with a procedure for making future amendments to it, and with a Charter of Rights.

The involvement of the courts in this issue began when the three provincial governments of Newfoundland, Quebec and Manitoba asked for rulings from their provincial Courts of Appeal on the constitutionality of the federal government's proposed action. Eventually, eight provincial governments opposed Ottawa's plan, while Ontario and New Brunswick supported it. In the House of Commons, the New Democratic Party decided to support the Liberal majority, but the Conservative party vigorously fought it. To end a successful parliamentary filibuster by the Tories in spring 1981, the Liberals agreed to refer the question of the constitutionality of their plan to the Supreme Court of Canada and to wait for the court's final decision before finalizing the resolution asking Britain to act.

The results of the lower court hearings on these matters were mixed. A majority of the Manitoba Court of Appeal and the Quebec Court of Appeal ruled in favour of Ottawa, but the Appeal Court of Newfoundland ruled unanimously in favour of the provinces.

The Supreme Court of Canada had before it the questions posed by the provinces and these earlier court decisions when it held its hearings in April and May 1981. The court's decisions were delivered in September 1981. They are included in full in this book.

THE ISSUES AND THE DECISIONS

In rendering their judgments on the questions asked of them, all nine Supreme Court judges agreed that the federal government's proposed action affected the rights and powers of the provinces. That was the issue posed in Question 1 by Manitoba and Newfoundland, and in Question A by Quebec.

The judges divided the other questions they had to answer into two issues, and their decisions on each of these matters were split. The first issue the Supreme Court dealt with was the legality of the federal government's proposed action — whether or not it contravenes an established law which the courts have the power to enforce. Chapters 1 and 2 contain the court decisions on this matter. Chapter 1 is the majority opinion in which seven judges, led by Chief Justice Bora Laskin, decide that Ottawa's action would be within the law. Chapter 2 is the minority opinion signed by two judges, whose view is that Ottawa's action would not be legal.

The second issue dealt with by the Supreme Court was the matter of constitutional conventions, specifically whether there is in Canada a constitutional convention which requires the consent of the provinces before a change that affects their rights and powers can be made in the constitution. All nine judges agreed that there are indeed constitutional conventions which operate in Canada, and they offer definitions of what a "convention" is. Chapter 3 is the majority opinion of six judges who ruled that Ottawa's proposed action would violate Canadian constitutional convention. Chapter 4 is the minority opinion of three whose position is that it would not.

One other matter which the Supreme Court was asked to rule on concerned Newfoundland. The question was whether the terms of union between Newfoundland and Canada could be altered without the approval of the provincial legislature or a provincial referendum. In Chapter 1, the Supreme Court explains its reasons for agreeing with the decision of the Newfoundland Court of Appeal that a legislative resolution or referendum is necessary.

WHY IN BOOK FORM?

Not many decisions of the Supreme Court are of such broad interest as these, or so important to the future of Canada. Their significance was reflected in the court's decision to allow, for the first time, television cameras into the courtroom on the day the verdicts were rendered. It also warranted, we concluded, the publication of the decisions in book form so they can be accessible to the many Canadians who regularly visit bookstores and use libraries. This offers wider, faster and more public access than the usual methods by which Supreme Court decisions are published in full and summarized, in many forms, in law reports and other materials found in law libraries.

These Supreme Court decisions offer a discussion of the nature of Canada's constitution, the country's relationship with Britain, the amending process, and the division of powers between Ottawa and the provinces. They will be central to the ongoing debate about the nature of the Canadian confederation. Between the majority and minority judgments on the two issues dealt with by the court, they offer very divergent views. These decisions offer the public an opportunity to aquaint itself with both sides of the debate on issues of vital public interest. Fortunately, the authors of these decisions wrote them in a way which makes them accessible to any reader. That is as it should be, since all Canadians should be deciding what kind of constitution this country should have.

A BRIEF READER'S GUIDE

For readers who are not familiar with the way court decisions are set out, and with their forms and terminologies, here is a brief guide.

The decisions arose out of referrals to provincial Courts of Appeal by three provincial governments. These governments posed questions which they asked the courts to answer. Manitoba asked three questions; Newfoundland put the same three questions to its court, and added a fourth on the specific matter of Newfoundland's status. The Quebec government posed two questions, each of which had two parts. Decisions on these questions were first handed down by each of the provincial courts. Those decisions are summarized in Chapter 1. Then the whole matter was referred to the Supreme Court, which reviewed the earlier decisions of the lower courts and made a final determination.

The questions put to the provincial courts are

repeated at the beginning of each of the four decisions. For easy reference, they are also reproduced in this book on pages xvii-xviii.

The Supreme Court divided the questions into two major issues. The first relates to the legality of the federal government's proposed course of action for unilateral patriation of the BNA Act and incorporation of an amending formula and a Charter of Rights. Chapter 1 states the majority decision on this issue. Seven judges, listed at the top of that decision, decided that Ottawa's proposed action was legal. Their ruling first sets out the history of how the matter came before the Supreme Court, summarizes the lower court decisions, presents the Supreme Court majority's own arguments and reasons, and concludes with their answers to the specific questions posed.

Chapter 2 is the minority decision on the same questions by Justices Martland and Ritchie. The two dissenting judges again set out the questions they are addressing (the same as the majority), give their reasons, and conclude with their answers.

The second issue dealt with by the Supreme Court was constitutional convention, and particularly whether Ottawa's proposed plan for unilateral patriation and amendment violates a Canadian constitutional convention. Chapter 3 is the decision of the majority of the court on that matter, beginning with the questions the court was asked, going on to define what a constitutional convention is and to discuss whether Ottawa's plan violates a convention, and ending with their precise answers to the questions posed. The majority ruled on this issue that Ottawa's actions would violate a constitutional convention.

Chapter 4 is the decision of the three judges who dissented on this issue. It follows the same structure as Chapter 3.

Once through the introductory material to each decision and into the substance of the matter, a reader not expert in constitutional law will find the judgments straightforward in their language and not difficult to follow. Only occasionally do the judges make use of mysterious legal terminology or shorthand. There are, for instance, abbreviations like "JA"; "Hall JA" means Appeal Judge Hall. References set out like "R.S.M. 1970 c. C-180" are to legal reference material and follow a standard form; that particular reference is to the Revised Statutes of Manitoba of 1970, chapter C-180. These references will be of interest mainly to specialists, but anyone who wants to follow them up will find the necessary reference materials in a law library.

THE JUDGES AND THEIR VOTING PATTERNS

The Supreme Court which heard these constitutional arguments and made these decisions was made up of six judges appointed by the Trudeau Liberal government, two appointed by the Conservative government of John Diefenbaker in the Fifties, and one appointed by Conservative prime minister Joe Clark. In its decisions, the court breaks down into three groups. There is a liberal wing of three judges who supported Ottawa on both issues; a conservative wing of two who supported the provinces on both issues; and a swing group of four, including the three Quebec judges. The swing group's votes went with the liberals to make a majority on the issue of legality and to the conservatives to make a majority with them on the issue of conventions.

The liberal wing of the court, which supported the federal government's position on both issues of legality and constitutional convention, was headed by Chief Justice Bora Laskin, and included Judge Willard Estey and Judge William McIntyre. Laskin was appointed to the Supreme Court in 1970 after a long career, first as a law professor at Osgoode Hall and the University of Toronto

VOTING PATTERNS
ON THE 1981 CONSTITUTIONAL DECISIONS

ISSUES	SUPREME COURT JUDGES		
	LIBERAL WING	*SWING GROUP*	*CONSERVATIVE WING*
	Laskin	Dickson	Ritchie
	Estey	Beetz	Martland
	McIntyre	Chouinard	
		Lamer	
Legality (Questions 1, 3, A and B (as a matter of law))	Ottawa	Ottawa	7-2 Provinces
Convention (Questions 2, B)	Ottawa	3-6 Provinces	Provinces

Law School, and then as a lower court judge. He was appointed Chief Justice in 1973 by Trudeau over the heads of more senior judges. He is widely respected as a constitutional scholar, and he holds strong centralist and civil-libertarian views close to Trudeau's.

Judge Estey was Chief Justice of Ontario for three years before being named to the Supreme Court in 1977. He is regarded as a civil libertarian, and often sides with Laskin on these matters.

Judge McIntyre was a lawyer in British Columbia before being named to the Supreme Court of B.C. in 1967. He was named to the Supreme Court of Canada by the Liberals in January 1979, just before the general election. He is also considered a liberal and a supporter of civil rights.

The conservative wing of the court, which supported the eight provincial governments in their opposition to Ottawa's plan, had two members, Roland Ritchie and Ronald Martland. Both were appointed by the Diefenbaker government. Ritchie, the only representative of the Maritimes in the court, was appointed in 1959. He has a mixed record on civil liberties, and has often been a swing vote on important issues.

Judge Martland, due to retire in 1982, is an Albertan whose record is pro-authority, pro-government, and not supportive of an entrenched charter of rights.

The four judges in the swing group were Brian Dickson from Manitoba, and Jean Beetz, Julien Chouinard and Antonio Lamer from Quebec. By voting with the liberal wing on the question of legality, these judges made the decision 7-2 in favour of Ottawa. By voting with the conservative wing on the matter of constitutional conventions, these judges made that decision 6-3 in favour of the provinces.

Judge Dickson practised law in Manitoba and then served on the bench for 10 years until his appointment by the Trudeau government to the Supreme Court in 1973.

Judge Dickson is usually considered to belong to the court's liberal wing, and steers a middle ground between the provinces and Ottawa.

Judge Beetz, the senior francophone of the court, is a constitutional scholar like Chief Justice Bora Laskin. He is a strong defender of provincial rights, and not a strong advocate of civil rights. A personal friend of Pierre Trudeau, he was an advisor to the prime minister in the period leading up to the 1971 Victoria conference. He was appointed by Trudeau to the court in 1974.

Judge Chouinard was appointed by Joe Clark in 1979. He had been Quebec's deputy minister of justice, a Conservative candidate in the 1968 federal election, and Quebec's top civil servant until his appointment to the Quebec Court of Appeal in 1975.

Judge Lamer was a criminal lawyer for several years and a judge in Quebec before going to the Law Reform Commission of Canada as vice-chairman in 1971. He returned to the bench in 1978, and was appointed by the Trudeau government to the Supreme Court in 1980.[1]

One result of the divergent views held by the judges of the Supreme Court of Canada is that, on these constitutional issues, they produced majority and minority decisions which reflected and argued their different positions.

The action of the swing group of four judges, joining the liberal wing on one issue and the conservative wing on the other, produced a result which both sides could claim as a victory. At the same time, it pushed the two sides towards negotiations which implicitly acknowledged the legitimacy which the court found in both their positions.

These Supreme Court decisions help clarify the nature of the Canadian constitution and, for that reason alone, are of continuing interest. At the same time, the Supreme Court itself has a role in the Canadian political process —

not just an academic one of analyzing and criticizing the issues, but an active one of intervening to shape the outcome of the political process. Canada's constitution is something we can all understand, debate, and take sides on in a knowledgeable and informed way. We don't have to rely on the second-hand — and very self-interested — interpretations and simplifications offered by the politicians involved. The proof of the matter is right here, in the texts of these 1981 Supreme Court decisions.

NOTE
1. This biographical information is from *The Globe and Mail*, 29 September 1981, p. D-2.

THE QUESTIONS

MANITOBA

1. If the amendments to the Constitution of Canada sought in the 'Proposed Resolution for a Joint Address to Her Majesty the Queen respecting the Constitution of Canada', or any of them, were enacted, would federal-provincial relationships or the powers, rights or privileges granted or secured by the Constitution of Canada to the provinces, their legislatures or governments be affected and, if so, in what respect or respects?

2. Is it a constitutional convention that the House of Commons and Senate of Canada will not request Her Majesty the Queen to lay before the Parliament of the United Kingdom of Great Britain and Northern Ireland a measure to amend the Constitution of Canada affecting federal-provincial relationships or the powers, rights or privileges granted or secured by the Constitution of Canada to the provinces, their legislatures or governments without first obtaining the agreement of the provinces?

3. Is the agreement of the provinces of Canada constitutionally required for amendment to the Constitution of Canada where such amendment affects federal-provincial relationships or alters the powers, rights or privileges granted or secured by the Constitution of Canada to the provinces, their legislatures or governments?

NEWFOUNDLAND

The same three questions as in Manitoba were asked in the Newfoundland Reference and, in addition, a fourth question was put in these terms:

4. If Part V of the proposed resolution referred to in question 1 is enacted and proclaimed into force could

(a) the Terms of Union, including terms 2 and 17 thereof contained in the Schedule to the British North America Act 1949 (12-13 George VI, c.22,(U.K.)), or

(b) section 3 of the British North America Act, 1871 (34-35 Victoria, c. 28) (U.K.)

be amended directly or indirectly pursuant to Part V without the consent of the Government, Legislature or a majority of the people of the Province of Newfoundland voting in a referendum held pursuant to Part V?

QUEBEC

In the Quebec Reference there was a different formulation, two questions being asked which read:

(Translation)

A. If the Canada Act and the Constitution Act 1981 should come into force and if they should be valid in all respects in Canada would they affect:

(i) the legislative competence of the provincial legislature in virtue of the Canadian Constitution?

(ii) the status or role of the provincial legislatures or governments within the Canadian Federation?

B. Does the Canadian Constitution empower, whether by statute, convention or otherwise, the Senate and the House of Commons of Canada to cause the Canadian Constitution to be amended without the consent of the provinces and in spite of the objection of several of them, in such a manner as to affect:

(i) the legislative competence of the provincial legislatures in virtue of the Canadian Constitution?

(ii) the status or role of the provincial legislatures or governments within the Canadian Federation?

THE ACTION, THE PARTIES AND COUNSEL

IN THE MATTER of an Act for expediting the decision of constitutional and other provincial questions; being Chapter C 180, C.C.S.M. AND IN THE MATTER of a Reference pursuant thereto by the Lieutenant Governor in Council to the Court of Appeal for Manitoba for hearing and consideration, the questions concerning the amendment of the Constitution of Canada as set out in Order in Council No. 1020/80.

THE ATTORNEY GENERAL OF MANITOBA
—and—
THE ATTORNEY GENERAL OF QUEBEC
THE ATTORNEY GENERAL OF NOVA SCOTIA
THE ATTORNEY GENERAL OF BRITISH COLUMBIA
THE ATTORNEY GENERAL OF PRINCE EDWARD ISLAND
THE ATTORNEY GENERAL OF SASKATCHEWAN
THE ATTORNEY GENERAL OF ALBERTA
THE ATTORNEY GENERAL OF NEWFOUNDLAND
FOUR NATIONS CONFEDERACY INC.
v.
THE ATTORNEY GENERAL OF CANADA
—and—
THE ATTORNEY GENERAL OF ONTARIO
THE ATTORNEY GENERAL OF NEW BRUNSWICK

CORAM:
The Right Honourable Bora Laskin, P.C., C.J.C.
The Hon. Mr. Justice Martland
The Hon. Mr. Justice Ritchie
The Hon. Mr. Justice Dickson
The Hon. Mr. Justice Beetz
The Hon. Mr. Justice Estey
The Hon. Mr. Justice McIntyre
The Hon. Mr. Justice Chouinard
The Hon. Mr. Justice Lamer

Appeal heard
    April 28, 29, 30 and May 1 and 4, 1981
Judgment pronounced
    September 28, 1981

Reasons on Questions 1 and 3 by
The Chief Justice
The Hon. Mr. Justice Dickson
The Hon. Mr. Justice Beetz
The Hon. Mr. Justice Estey
The Hon. Mr. Justice McIntyre
The Hon. Mr. Justice Chouinard
The Hon. Mr. Justice Lamer

Reasons concurring on Question 1 and dissenting on Question 3 by
The Hon. Mr. Justice Martland
The Hon. Mr. Justice Ritchie

Reasons on Question 2 by
The Hon. Mr. Justice Martland
The Hon. Mr. Justice Ritchie
The Hon. Mr. Justice Dickson
The Hon. Mr. Justice Beetz
The Hon. Mr. Justice Chouinard
The Hon. Mr. Justice Lamer

Dissenting reasons on Question 2 by
The Chief Justice
The Hon. Mr. Justice Estey
The Hon. Mr. Justice McIntyre

Counsel at hearing:
For the appellant:
Mr. A. Kerr Twaddle, Q.C.
Mr. Douglas A. J. Schmeiser
Mr. Brian F. Squair

For the Attorney General of Quebec
Mr. Colin K. Irving
Mr. Georges Emery, Q.C.
Mr. Lucien Bouchard
Mr. Peter S. Martin

For the Attorney General of Nova Scotia
Mr. Gordon F. Coles, Q.C.
Mr. Reinhold M. Enders
Ms. Mollie Dunsmuir

For the Attorney General of British Columbia
Mr. D.M.M. Goldie, Q.C.
Mr. E.R.A. Edwards
Mr. C.F. Willms

For the Attorney General of Prince Edward Island
Mr. Ian W. H. Bailey

For the Attorney General of Saskatchewan
Mr. K. Lysyk, Q.C.
Mr. Darryl Bogdasavich
Mr. John D. Whyte

For the Attorney General of Alberta
Mr. Ross W. Paisley, Q.C.
Mr. William Henkel, Q.C.

For the Attorney General of Newfoundland
Mr. John J. O'Neill, Q.C.
Mr. John J. Ashley
Mr. James L. Thistle

For the Four Nations Confederacy Inc.
Mr. D'Arcy C. H. McCaffrey, Q.C.

For the respondent:
Mr. J. J. Robinette, Q.C.
Mr. John Scollin, Q.C.
Mr. Michel Robert

For the Attorney General of Ontario
Mr. Roy McMurtry, Q.C.
Mr. D. W. Mundell, Q.C.
Mr. John Cavarzan, Q.C.
Ms. Lorraine E. Weinrib

For the Attorney General of New Brunswick
Mr. Alan D. Reid
Mr. Alfred R. Landry, Q.C.

IN THE MATTER of Section 6 of The Judicature Act,
R.S.N. 1970, c. 187 as amended AND IN THE MATTER of a
Reference by the Lieutenant-Governor in Council concern-
ing the effect and validity of the amendments to the Consti-
tution of Canada sought in the 'Proposed Resolution for a
Joint Address to Her Majesty The Queen respecting the
Constitution of Canada'

THE ATTORNEY GENERAL OF CANADA
—and—
THE ATTORNEY GENERAL OF ONTARIO
THE ATTORNEY GENERAL OF NEW BRUNSWICK
 v.

THE ATTORNEY GENERAL OF NEWFOUNDLAND
—and—
THE ATTORNEY GENERAL OF QUEBEC
THE ATTORNEY GENERAL OF NOVA SCOTIA
THE ATTORNEY GENERAL OF MANITOBA
THE ATTORNEY GENERAL OF BRITISH COLUMBIA
THE ATTORNEY GENERAL OF PRINCE EDWARD IS-
LAND
THE ATTORNEY GENERAL OF SASKATCHEWAN
THE ATTORNEY GENERAL OF ALBERTA
FOUR NATONS CONFEDERACY INC.
CORAM:
The Right Honourable Bora Laskin, P.C., C.J.C.
The Hon. Mr. Justice Martland
The Hon. Mr. Justice Ritchie
The Hon. Mr. Justice Dickson
The Hon. Mr. Justice Beetz
The Hon. Mr. Justice Estey
The Hon. Mr. Justice McIntyre
The Hon. Mr. Justice Chouinard
The Hon. Mr. Justice Lamer
Appeal heard
 May 4, 1981
Judgment pronounced
 September 28, 1981

Reasons on Questions 1, 3 and 4 by
The Chief Justice
The Hon. Mr. Justice Dickson
The Hon. Mr. Justice Beetz
The Hon. Mr. Justice Estey
The Hon. Mr. Justice McIntyre
The Hon. Mr. Justice Chouinard
The Hon. Mr. Justice Lamer

Reasons concurring on Questions 1 and 4 and dissenting on
Question 3 by
The Hon. Mr. Justice Martland
The Hon. Mr. Justice Ritchie

Reasons on Question 2 by
The Hon. Mr. Justice Martland
The Hon. Mr. Justice Ritchie
The Hon. Mr. Justice Beetz
The Hon. Mr. Justice Chouinard
The Hon. Mr. Justice Lamer

Dissenting reasons on Question 2 by
The Chief Justice
The Hon. Mr. Justice Estey
The Hon. Mr. Justice McIntyre

Counsel at hearing:
For the appellant:
Mr. Clive Wells, Q.C.
Mr. Barry Strayer, Q.C.
Mrs. Barbara Reed

For the Attorney General of Ontario
Mr. Roy McMurtry, Q.C.
Mr. D. W. Mundell, Q.C.
Mr. John Cavarzan, Q.C.
Ms. Lorraine E. Weinrib

For the Attorney General of New Brunswick
Mr. Alan D. Reid
Mr. Alfred R. Landry, Q.C.

For the respondent:
Mr. John J. O'Neill, Q.C.
Mr. John J. Ashley
Mr. James L. Thistle

For the Attorney General of Quebec
Mr. Colin K. Irving
Mr. Georges Emery, Q.C.
Mr. Lucien Bouchard
Mr. Peter S. Martin

For the Attorney General of Nova Scotia
Mr. Gordon F. Coles, Q.C.
Mr. Reinhold M. Enders
Ms. Mollie Dunsmuir

For the Attorney General of Manitoba
Mr. A. Kerr Twaddle, Q.C.
Mr. Douglas A. J. Schmeiser
Mr. Brian F. Squair

For the Attorney General of British Columbia
Mr. D. M. M. Goldie, Q.C.
Mr. E. R. A. Edwards
Mr. C. F. Willms

For the Attorney General of Prince Edward Island
Mr. Ian W. H. Bailey

For the Attorney General of Saskatchewan
Mr. K. Lysyk, Q.C.
Mr. Darryl Bogdasavich
Mr. John D. Whyte

For the Attorney General of Alberta
Mr. Ross W. Paisley, Q.C.
Mr. William Henkel, Q.C.

Four Four Nations Confederacy Inc.
Mr. D'Arcy C. H. McCaffrey, Q.C.

IN THE MATTER of a Reference to the Court of Appeal
of Quebec relative to a draft Resolution containing a joint
address to Her Majesty The Queen concerning the Constitution of Canada

THE ATTORNEY GENERAL OF QUEBEC
 (Appellant/Respondent)
 —and—
THE ATTORNEY GENERAL OF CANADA
 (Respondent/Appellant)
 —and—
THE ATTORNEY GENERAL OF NOVA SCOTIA
THE ATTORNEY GENERAL OF MANITOBA
THE ATTORNEY GENERAL OF BRITISH COLUMBIA
THE ATTORNEY GENERAL OF PRINCE EDWARD IS-
LAND
THE ATTORNEY GENERAL OF SASKATCHEWAN
THE ATTORNEY GENERAL OF ALBERTA

THE ATTORNEY GENERAL OF NEWFOUNDLAND
FOUR NATIONS CONFEDERACY INC.
(Intervenants supporting the Attorney General of Quebec)

THE ATTORNEY GENERAL OF ONTARIO
THE ATTORNEY GENERAL OF NEW BRUNSWICK
(Intervenants supporting the Attorney General of Canada)

CORAM:
The Right Honourable Bora Laskin, P.C., C.J.C.
The Hon. Mr. Justice Martland
The Hon. Mr. Justice Ritchie
The Hon. Mr. Justice Dickson
The Hon. Mr. Justice Beetz
The Hon. Mr. Justice Estey
The Hon. Mr. Justice McIntyre
The Hon. Mr. Justice Chouinard
The Hon. Mr. Justice Lamer

Appeal heard
    May 4, 1981
Judgment pronounced
    September 28, 1981

Reasons on Question A and the legal aspect of Question B
by
The Chief Justice
The Hon. Mr. Justice Dickson
The Hon. Mr. Justice Beetz
The Hon. Mr. Justice Estey
The Hon. Mr. Justice McIntyre
The Hon. Mr. Justice Chouinard
The Hon. Mr. Justice Lamer

Reasons concurring on Question A and dissenting on the legal aspect of Question B by
The Hon. Mr. Justice Martland
The Hon. Mr. Justice Ritchie
Reasons on the conventional aspect of Question B by
The Hon. Mr. Justice Martland
The Hon. Mr. Justice Ritchie
The Hon. Mr. Justice Dickson
The Hon. Mr. Justice Beetz
The Hon. Mr. Justice Chouinard
The Hon. Mr. Justice Lamer

Dissenting reasons on the conventional aspect of Question B
by
The Chief Justice
The Hon. Mr. Justice Estey
The Hon. Mr. Justice McIntyre

Counsel at hearing:
For the appellant:
Mr. Colin K. Irving
Mr. Georges Emery, Q.C.
Mr. Lucien Bouchard
Mr. Peter S. Martin

For the Attorney General of Nova Scotia
Mr. Gordon F. Coles, Q.C.
Mr. Reinhold M. Enders
Ms. Mollie Dunsmuir

For the Attorney General of Manitoba
Mr. A. Kerr Twaddle, Q.C.
Mr. Douglas A. J. Schmeiser
Mr. Brian F. Squair

For the Attorney General of British Columbia
Mr. D. M. M. Goldie, Q.C.
Mr. E. R. A. Edwards
Mr. C. F. Willms

For the Attorney General of Prince Edward Island
Mr. Ian Q. H. Bailey
For the Attorney General of Saskatchewan
Mr. K. Lysyk, Q.C.
Mr. Darryl Bogdasavich
Mr. John D. Whyte

For the Attorney General of Alberta
Mr. Ross W. Paisley, Q.C.
Mr. William Henkel, Q.C.

For Four Nations Confederacy Inc.
Mr. D'Arcy C. H. McCaffrey, Q.C.

For the respondent:
Mr. Michel Robert
Mr. Raynold Langlois
Mr. Louis Reynolds

For the Attorney General of Ontario
Mr. Roy McMurtry, Q.C.
Mr. D. W. Mundell, Q.C.
Mr. John Cavarzan, Q.C.
Ms. Lorraine E. Weinrib

For the Attorney General of New Brunswick
Mr. Alan D. Reid
Mr. Alfred R. Landry, Q.C.

1 LEGALITY: THE MAJORITY DECISION

BY CHIEF JUSTICE LASKIN AND JUDGES DICKSON, BEETZ, ESTEY, McINTYRE, CHOUINARD AND LAMER

IN THE MATTER of an Act for expediting the decision of constitutional and other provincial questions, being R.S.M. 1970, c. C-180

AND IN THE MATTER of a Reference pursuant thereto by the Lieutenant Governor in Council to the Court of Appeal for Manitoba for hearing and consideration, the questions concerning the amendment of the Constitution of Canada as set out in Order in Council No. 1020/80

THE ATTORNEY GENERAL OF MANITOBA
(Appellant)

—and—

THE ATTORNEY GENERAL OF QUEBEC
THE ATTORNEY GENERAL OF NOVA SCOTIA
THE ATTORNEY GENERAL OF BRITISH COLUMBIA
THE ATTORNEY GENERAL OF PRINCE EDWARD IS-
LAND
THE ATTORNEY GENERAL OF SASKATCHEWAN
THE ATTORNEY GENERAL OF ALBERTA
THE ATTORNEY GENERAL OF NEWFOUNDLAND
FOUR NATIONS CONFEDERACY INC.
(Intervenors)

—v—

THE ATTORNEY GENERAL OF CANADA
(Respondent)

—and—

1

THE ATTORNEY GENERAL OF ONTARIO
THE ATTORNEY GENERAL OF NEW BRUNSWICK
(Intervenors)

IN THE MATTER of Section 6 of The Judicature Act,
R.S.N. 1970, c. 187 as amended,
AND IN THE MATTER OF a Reference by the Lieutenant-Governor in Council concerning the effect and validity
of the amendments to the Constitution of Canada sought in
the 'Proposed Resolution for a Joint Address to Her Majesty
The Queen respecting the Constitution of Canada'

THE ATTORNEY GENERAL OF CANADA
(Appellant)
—and—

THE ATTORNEY GENERAL OF ONTARIO
THE ATTORNEY GENERAL OF NEW BRUNSWICK
(Intervenors)
—v—

THE ATTORNEY GENERAL OF NEWFOUNDLAND
(Respondent)
—and—

THE ATTORNEY GENERAL OF QUEBEC
THE ATTORNEY GENERAL OF NOVA SCOTIA
THE ATTORNEY GENERAL OF BRITISH COLUMBIA
THE ATTORNEY GENERAL OF PRINCE EDWARD IS-
LAND
THE ATTORNEY GENERAL OF SASKATCHEWAN
THE ATTORNEY GENERAL OF ALBERTA
FOUR NATIONS CONFEDERACY INC.
(Intervenors)

AND IN THE MATTER of a Reference to the Court of
Appeal of Quebec relative to a draft Resolution containing a
joint address to Her Majesty The Queen concerning the Constitution of Canada

2

THE ATTORNEY GENERAL OF QUEBEC
(Appellant/Respondent)
—and—

THE ATTORNEY GENERAL OF CANADA
(Respondent/Appellant)
—and—

THE ATTORNEY GENERAL OF MANITOBA
THE ATTORNEY GENERAL OF BRITISH COLUMBIA
THE ATTORNEY GENERAL OF PRINCE EDWARD IS-
LAND
THE ATTORNEY GENERAL OF ALBERTA
THE ATTORNEY GENERAL OF NOVA SCOTIA
THE ATTORNEY GENERAL OF SASKATCHEWAN
FOUR NATIONS CONFEDERACY INC.
(Intervenors supporting the Attorney General of Quebec)

—and—

THE ATTORNEY GENERAL OF ONTARIO
THE ATTORNEY GENERAL OF NEW BRUNSWICK
(Intervenors supporting the Attorney General of Canada)

CORAM:
The Chief Justice and Martland, Ritchie, Dickson, Beetz,
Estey, McIntyre, Chouinard and Lamer JJ.

THE CHIEF JUSTICE and DICKSON, BEETZ, ESTEY,
McINTYRE, CHOUINARD and LAMER JJ.

I

Three appeals as of right are before this Court, concerning in the main common issues. They arise out of three References made, respectively, to the Manitoba Court of Appeal, to the Newfoundland Court of Appeal and to the Quebec Court of Appeal by the respective Governments of the
three Provinces.

Three questions were posed in the Manitoba Reference, as follows:

1. If the amendments to the Constitution of Canada sought in the 'Proposed Resolution for a Joint Address to Her Majesty the Queen respecting the Constitution of Canada', or any of them, were enacted, would federal-provincial relationships or the powers, rights or privileges granted or secured by the Constitution of Canada to the provinces, their legislatures or governments be affected and if so, in what respect or respects?

2. Is it a constitutional convention that the House of Commons and Senate of Canada will not request Her Majesty the Queen to lay before the Parliament of the United Kingdom of Great Britain and Northern Ireland a measure to amend the Constitution of Canada affecting federal-provincial relationships or the powers, rights or privileges granted or secured by the Constitution of Canada to the provinces, their legislatures or governments without first obtaining the agreement of the provinces?

3. Is the agreement of the provinces of Canada constitutionally required for amendment to the Constitution of Canada where such amendment affects federal-provincial relationships or alters the powers, rights or privileges granted or secured by the Constitution of Canada to the provinces, their legislatures or governments?

The same three questions were asked in the Newfoundland Reference and, in addition, a fourth question was put in these terms:

4. If Part V of the proposed resolution referred to in question 1 is enacted and proclaimed into force could

(a) the Terms of Union, including terms 2 and 17 thereof contained in the Schedule to the British North America Act 1949 (12-13 George VI, c. 22 (U.K.)), or

(b) section 3 of the British North America Act, 1871 (34-35 Victoria, c. 28) (U.K.)

be amended directly or indirectly pursuant to Part V without the consent of the Government, Legislature or a majority of the people of the Province of Newfoundland voting in a referendum held pursuant to Part V?

In the Quebec Reference there was a different formulation, two questions being asked which read:

(TRANSLATION)

A. If the Canada Act and the Constitution Act 1981 should come into force and if they should be valid in all respects in Canada would they affect:

(i) the legislative competence of the provincial legislature in virtue of the Canadian Constitution?

B. Does the Canadian Constitution empower, whether by stature, convention or otherwise, the Senate and the House of Commons of Canada to cause the Canadian Constitution to be amended without the consent of the provinces and in spite of the objection of several of them, in such a manner as to affect:

(i) the legislative competence of the provincial legislatures in virtue of the Canadian Constitution?

(ii) the status or role of the provincial legislatures or governments within the Canadian Federation?

The answers given by the Judges of the Manitoba Court of Appeal, each of whom wrote reasons, are as follows:

Freedman C.J.M.:
   Question 1 — Not answered, because it is tentative and premature.
   Question 2 — No
   Question 3 — No

Hall, J.A.:
   Question 1 — Not answered because it is not appropriate for judicial response, and, in any event, the question is speculative and premature.
   Question 2 — Not answered because it is not appropriate for judicial response.
   Question 3 — No, because there is no legal requirement of provincial agreement to amendment of the Constitution as asserted in the question.

Mates, J.A.:
   Question 1 — Not answered, because it is speculative and premature.
   Question 2 — No
   Question 3 — No

O'Sullivan, J.A.:
   Question 1 — Yes, as set out in reasons.
   Question 2 — The constitutional convention referred to has not been established as a matter simply of precedent; it is, however, a constitutional principle binding in law that the House of Commons and Senate of Canada should not request Her Majesty the Queen to lay before the Parliament of the United Kingdom of Great Britain and Northern Ireland any measure to amend the Constitution of Canada affecting federal-provincial relationships or the powers, rights or privileges granted or secured by the Constitution of Canada to the provinces, their legislatures of governments without first obtaining the agreement of the provinces.
   Question 3 — Yes, as set out in reasons.

Huband, J.A.:
   Question 1 — Yes
   Question 2 — No
   Question 3 — Yes.

The Newfoundland Court of Appeal, in reasons of the Court concurred in by all three Judges who sat on the Reference, answered all three questions common to the Manitoba Reference in the affirmative. The Court answered the four questions in this way:

5

(1) By Sec. 3 of the British North America Act, 1871, Term 2 of the Terms of Union cannot now be changed without the consent of the Newfoundland Legislature.

(2) By Sec. 43 of the 'Constitution Act', as it now reads, none of the Terms of Union can be changed without the consent of the Newfoundland Legislative Assembly.

(3) Both of these sections can be changed by the amending formulae prescribed in Sec. 41 and the Terms of Union could then be changed without the consent of the Newfoundland Legislature.

(4) If the amending formula under Sec. 42 is utilized, both of these sections can be changed by a referendum held pursuant to the provisions of Sec. 42. In this event, the Terms of Union could then be changed without the consent of the Newfoundland Legislature, but not without the consent of the majority of the Newfoundland people voting in a referendum.

The Quebec Court of Appeal, in reasons delivered by each of the five Judges who sat on the Reference, answered the two questions submitted to it as follows:

(TRANSLATION)

Question A (i) yes (unanimously)
(ii) yes (unanimously)
Question B (i) yes (Bisson J.A. dissenting would answer no)
(ii) yes (Bisson J.A. dissenting would answer no)

II

The References in question here were prompted by the opposition of six Provinces, later joined by two others, to a proposed Resolution which was published on October 2, 1980 and intended for submission to the House of Commons and as well to the Senate of Canada. It contained an address to be presented to Her Majesty The Queen in right of the United Kingdom respecting what may generally be referred to as the Constitution of Canada. The address laid before the House of Commons on October 6, 1980, was in these terms:

To the Queen's Most Excellent Majesty:
Most Gracious Sovereign:
We, Your Majesty's loyal subjects, the House of Commons of Canada in Parliament assembled, respectfully approach Your Majesty, requesting that you may graciously be pleased to cause to be laid before the Parliament of the United Kingdom a measure containing the recitals and clauses hereinafter set forth:

6

An Act to give effect to a request by the Senate and House of Commons of Canada

Whereas Canada has requested and consented to the enactment of an Act of the Parliament of the United Kingdom to give effect to the provisions hereinafter set forth and the Senate and the House of Commons of Canada in Parliament assembled have submitted an address to Her Majesty requesting that Her Majesty may graciously be pleased to cause a Bill to be laid before the Parliament of the United Kingdom for that purpose.

Be it therefore enacted by the Queen's Most Excellent Majesty, by and with the advice and consent of the Lords Spiritual and Temporal, and Commons, in this present Parliament assembled, and by the authority of the same, as follows:

1. The *Constitution Act, 1981* set out in Schedule B to this Act is hereby enacted for and shall have the force of law in Canada and shall come into force as provided in that Act.

2. No Act of Parliament of the United Kingdom passed after the *Constitution Act, 1981* comes into force shall extend to Canada as part of its law.

3. So far as it is not contained in Schedule B, the French version of this Act is set out in Schedule A to this Act and has the same authority in Canada as the English version thereof.

4. This Act may be cited as the *Canada Act*.

It will be noticed that included in the terms of the address are the words "cause to be laid before the Parliament of the United Kingdom" and that they are reflected in question B put before the Quebec Court of Appeal. The proposed Resolution, as the terms of the address indicate, includes a statute which, in turn, has appended to it another statute providing for the patriation of the *British North America Act* (and a consequent change of name), with an amending procedure, and a *Charter of Rights and Freedoms* including a range of provisions (to be entrenched against legislative invasion) which it is unnecessary to enumerate. The proposed Resolution carried the approval of only two Provinces, Ontario and New Brunswick, expressed by their respective Governments. The opposition of the others, save Saskatchewan, was based on their assertion that both conventionally and legally the consent of all the Provinces was required for the address to go forward to Her Majesty with the appended statutes. Although there was general agreement on the desirability of patriation with an amending procedure, agreement could not be reached at conferences preceding the introduction of the proposed Resolution into the House of Commons, either on the constituents of such a procedure or on the formula to be embodied therein, or on the inclusion of a *Charter of Rights*.

The References to the respective Courts of Appeal were made and the hearings on the questions asked were held before the proposed Resolution was adopted. This fact underlays the unwillingness of Judges in the Manitoba Court of Appeal to answer question 1; changes might be made to the proposed Resolution in the course of debate and hence the assertion of prematurity.

The proposed Resolution, as adopted by the House of Commons on April 23, 1981 and the Senate on April 24, 1981, achieved its final form (there were but a few amendments to the original proposal) almost on the eve of the hearings in this Court on the three appeals. Indeed, the opinions of the Courts in all three References were given and certified before the ultimate adoption of the proposed Resolution. The result of its adoption by the Senate and by the House of Commons was to change the position of the Attorney General of Canada and of his two supporting intervenors on the propriety of answering question 1 in the Manitoba and Newfoundland References. He abandoned his initial contention that the question should not be answered.

III

The Reference legislation under which the various questions were put to the three Courts of Appeal is in wide terms. The Manitoba legislation, *An Act for Expediting the Decision of Constitutional and other Provincial Questions*, R.S.M. 1970, c. C-180 provides in s. 2 that the Lieutenant-Governor in Council may refer to the Court of Queen's

8

Bench or a Judge thereof or to the Court of Appeal or a Judge thereof for hearing or consideration "any matter which he thinks fit to refer." *The Newfoundland Judicature Act,* R.S. Nfld. 1970, c. 187, s. 6, as amended, similarly provides for a reference by the Lieutenant-Governor in Council to the Court of Appeal of "any matter which he thinks fit to refer." *The Court of Appeal Reference Act,* R.S.Q. 1977, c. R-23, s. 1 authorizes the Government of Quebec to refer to the Court of Appeal for hearing and consideration "any question which it deems expedient." The scope of the authority in each case is wide enough to saddle the respective Courts with the determination of questions which may not be justiciable and there is no doubt that those Courts, and this Court on appeal, have a discretion to refuse to answer such questions.

In the appeals now before this Court, it will have been noticed that three members of the Manitoba Court of Appeal refused to answer the first question before that Court as being tentative and premature or speculative and premature, and one of those Judges, Hall J.A., refused to answer the second question as not being appropriate for judicial response. As has already been noted, the adoption of the proposed Resolution by the Senate and House of Commons changed the position of the Attorney General of Canada who conceded in this Court that it was answerable. There is no doubt in this Court that since the first question in the Manitoba and Newfoundland References and question A in the Quebec Reference concern the construction of a document, especially one said to be in its final form, a justiciable issue is raised.

There is equally no doubt that the third question in those two References and question B in the Quebec Reference raise justiciable issues and, clearly, they must be answered when they raise questions of law. The different formulation of question B in the Quebec Reference, addressed to the authority of the federal House of convention, statute or otherwise to cause the Constitution to be amended (as proposed by the Resolution) without the consent of the Provinces, combines issues raised separately in question 2 and 3 in the other References.

9

IV

A summary of the views expressed in the Courts below on the various questions before them may usefully be set out at this point.

In the Manitoba Court of Appeal, the Chief Justice, Hall and Matas JJ.A. declined to answer question 1 because they felt the question was speculative and premature. O'Sullivan and Hubband JJ.A. in dissent each answered question 1 in the affirmative.

The Chief Justice, Matas and Huband JJ.A. answered question 2 in the negative. The Chief Justice canvassed previous amendments, and on that basis decided that no convention of provincial consent existed. Huband J.A. concurred with the Chief Justice. Matas J.A. also concurred, and went on to point out the numerous undefined and uncertain aspects of the alleged convention. Hall J.A. declined to answer question 2, being of the opinion that conventions were in the realm of politics and inappropriate for judicial consideration. O'Sullivan J.A. in dissent, declined to find any convention in precedent, but nonetheless stated that there was a "constitutional principle" requiring provincial consent.

Question 3 was answered in the negative by the Chief Justice, Hall and Matas JJ.A. Any "crystallization" of a convention was denied, as was the allegation of provincial "sovereignty". The Chief Justice analyzed and rejected the "compact theory" as a source of legal obligation. He was further of the view that the "sovereignty" contended for by the Provinces did not flow from the legislative supremacy granted by s. 92 of the *British North America Act*, but rather from something in the nature of an inherent right flowing from the fact of union. As such, it bore a direct relationship to the "compact theory," and was untenable. Hall J.A. unequivocally rejected the "compact theory" also, and denied that provincial supremacy within s. 92 created a legal requirement of provincial consent to constitutional amendment. Matas J.A. noted that the *Statute of Westminster, 1931*, gave the Provinces no new powers over amendment, and he also set out various limitations upon provincial legislative supremacy. O'Sullivan J.A. in dissent discussed and accepted the "compact theory", and further held that provincial sovereignty within s. 92 made it illegal for anyone to interfere with that sovereignty without provincial consent. Huband J.A. agreed, without expressing any opinion on the "compact theory." He was of the view that the Crown in these matters must rely on the advice of its provincial ministers. Further, he said that the United Kingdom Parliament is a "bare legislative trustee" for both the Provinces and the federal Parliament.

The Court of Appeal of Newfoundland began with question 3. It stressed the *Statute of Westminster* and the discussions leading to its passage, found that the United Kingdom had renounced all legislative sovereignty over Canada, and acts as a "bare legislative trustee" of the provincial legislatures and the federal Parliament. The Provinces, it said, were "autonomous communities", and the United Kingdom Parliament could not pass an amendment over their objections.

As to question 2, the Court analyzed the precedents and various positions of political figures. Stress was placed upon the 1965 federal White Paper on "The Amendment of the Constitution of Canada," and on the few occasions when provincial consent was obtained. The Court concluded that the direction of constitutional thinking has been towards the recognition of the right of the Provinces to be consulted, and answered question 2 in the affirmative.

Addressing question 1 in broad terms, the Court concluded it clearly must be answered in the affirmative.

Question 4, particular to the Newfoundland Reference, concerned the exact effect of the proposed amending formula upon the Terms of Union on which Newfoundland entered Confederation. The Court gave a complex answer which has already been quoted.

The Quebec Court of Appeal was in general faced with the same questions that were before the other Courts although phrased in a different way. All five members of the Court delivered reasons.

The Court unanimously answered question A in the affirmative. Four members of the Court answered question B in the affirmative, Bisson J.A. dissenting. As to question B, the Chief Justice of Quebec rejected any convention of provincial consent, and noted rather that any convention was in favour of the federal Parliament alone proceeding by joint resolution. The effect of the *Statute of Westminster* was simply to leave the legal power to amend the Constitution in the United Kingdom Parliament.

Owen J.A. stated that although the resolution was not specifically authorized by statute, the inherent power of Parliament justified the action. He rejected the "sovereignty", convention and "compact theory" arguments by reference to the reasons of Turgeon J.A. He noted that the provincial argument was weakened by the fact that Canada is not "the theoretical ideal confederation contemplated by text-book writers."

Turgeon J.A. affirmed that the power to amend before 1931 was in the United Kingdom Parliament, and the Statute of Westminster changed nothing. He listed the various fetters on provincial legislative supremacy, and noted that only the federal Parliament could act extra-territorially. After a lengthy analysis of previous amendments, he denied the existence of any convention of provincial consent. He also held the "compact theory" to be without historical or legal support.

Belanger J.A. doubted whether a resolution, as a matter of internal Parliamentary procedure, was susceptible to review by a court. Nonetheless, he answered question B in the affirmative, concurring with the Chief Justice and Turgeon J.A., and asking rhetorically whether it was the "essence of a federal union" that it remain stagnant and incapable of evolution in the face of perhaps only one provincial objection.

Bisson J.A. dissented on question B, and characterized the Resolution as a "quasi-legislative" act. In upholding provincial "sovereignty," he stressed the conferences and resolutions which preceded Confederation and which were given "legislative sanction" in the *British North America Act*. Canada, he held, was a "quasi-federation." Although provincial sovereignty was limited in some ways, nonetheless, the federal Parliament could not proceed alone. This, he said, was borne out by past practice.

V

The reasons which now follow deal with questions 1 and 3 in the Manitoba and Newfoundland References, with question 4 in the Newfoundland reference, with question A in the Quebec Reference, and with question B in that Reference in its legal aspect. Question 2 in the Manitoba and Newfoundland References and question B in the Quebec Reference in its comparable conventional aspect are dealt with in separate reasons.

VI

On the footing of the adopted Resolution, the Attorney General of Canada agrees that question 1 in the Manitoba and Newfoundland References and question A in the Quebec Reference should be answered in the affirmative as is asserted by the Attorneys General of Manitoba, Newfoundland and Quebec. Certainly, it is plain that under the terms of the enactments proposed in the Resolution, the legislative powers of the provincial Legislatures would be affected, indeed, limited by the *Charter of Rights and Freedoms*. The limitations of the proposed *Charter of Rights and Freedoms* on legislative power apply both at the federal level and the provincial level. This does not, however, alter the fact that there is an intended suppression of provincial legislative power. Moreover, the enhancement of provincial legislative authority under some provisions of the proposed enactment, as for example, in respect of resource control, including interprovincial export, (albeit subject to federal paramountcy) and in respect of taxing power does not alter the fact that there is an effect on existing federal-provincial relationships under these and other provisions of the draft statute intended for submission to enactment by the Parliament of the United Kingdom.

The simple answer "yes" to question 1 and question A answers both of them sufficiently, even though question 1 asks also "in what respect or respects" would federal-provincial relationships and provincial powers, rights or privileges be affected. Counsel were agreed that it would carry them and the Court into considerable exposition of detail if this aspect of question 1 were to be explored; for the time being, and affirmative answer to the primary issue in the question would satisfy all concerned.

VII

Coming now to question 3 in the Manitoba and New-foundland References and part B (on its legal side) in the Quebec Reference. By reason of the use of the words "constitutionally required" in question 3, the question imports both legal and conventional issues, and as the latter are dealt with in separate reasons, what follows is concerned only with the legal side of question 3 in the Manitoba and Newfoundland References and part B (on its legal side) in the Quebec Reference, which meets the submissions of all counsel on this issue.

There are two broad aspects to the matter under discussion which divide into a number of separate issues: (1) the authority of the two federal Houses to proceed by Resolution where provincial powers and federal-provincial relationships are thereby affected and (2) the role or authority of the Parliament of the United Kingdom to act on the Resolution. The first point concerns the need of legal power to initiate the process in Canada; the second concerns legal power or want of it in the Parliament of the United Kingdom to act on the resolution when it does not carry the consent of the Provinces.

The submission of the eight Provinces which invites this Court to consider the position of the British Parliament is based on the *Statute of Westminster, 1931* in its application to Canada. The submission is that the effect of the Statute is to qualify the authority of the British Parliament to act on the federal Resolution without previous provincial consent where provincial powers and interests are thereby affected, as they plainly are here. This issue will be examined later in these reasons.

Two observations are pertinent here. First, we have the anomaly that although Canada has international recognition as an independent, autonomous and self-governing state, as, for example, a founding member of the United Nations, and through membership in other international associations of sovereign states, yet it suffers from an internal deficiency in the absence of legal power to alter or amend the essential distributive arrangements under which legal authority is exercised in the country, whether at the federal or provincial level. When a country has been in existence as an operating federal state for more than a century, the task of introducing a legal mechanism that will thereafter remove the anomaly undoubtedly raises a profound problem. Secondly, the authority of the British Parliament or its practices and conventions are not matters upon which this Court would presume to pronounce.

The proposition was advanced on behalf of the Attorney General of Manitoba that a convention may crystallize into law and that the requirement of provincial consent to the kind of Resolution that we have here, although in origin political, has become a rule of law. (No firm position was taken on whether the consent must be that of the Governments or that of the Legislatures.)

In our view, this is not so. No instance of an explicit recognition of a convention as having matured into a rule of law was produced. The very nature of a convention, as political in inception and as depending on a consistent course of political recognition by those for whose benefit and to whose detriment (if any) the convention developed over a considerable period of time is inconsistent with its legal enforcement.

The attempted assimilation of the growth of a convention to the growth of the common law is misconceived. The latter is the product of judicial effort, based on justiciable issues which have attained legal formulation and are subject to modification and even reversal by the Courts which gave them birth when acting within their role in the State in obedience to statutes or constitutional directives. No such parental role is played by the Courts with respect to conventions.

It was urged before us that a host of cases have given legal force to conventions. This is an overdrawn proposition. One case in which direct recognition and enforcement of a convention was sought is *Madzimbamuto v. Lardner-Burke*, (1969) 1 A.C. 645. There the Privy Council rejected the assertion that a convention formally recognized by the

United Kingdom as established, namely, that it would not legislate for Southern Rhodesia on matters within the competence of the latter's legislature without its government's consent, could not be overriden by British legislation made applicable to Southern Rhodesia after the unilateral declaration of independence by the latter's government. Speaking for the Privy Council, Lord Reid pointed out that although the convention was a very important one, "it had no legal effect in limiting the legal power of Parliament" (at p. 723). And, again (at the same page):

It is often said that it would be unconstitutional for the United Kingdom Parliament to do certain things, meaning that the moral, political and other reasons against doing them are so strong that most people would regard it as highly improper if Parliament did these things. But that does not mean that it is beyond the power of Parliament to do such things. If parliament chose to do any of them the courts could not hold the Act of Parliament invalid. It may be that it would have been thought, before 1965, that it would be unconstitutional to disregard this convention. But it may also be that the unilateral Declaration of Independence released the United Kingdom from any obligation to observe the convention. Their Lordships in declaring the law are not concerned with these matters. They are only concerned with the legal powers of Parliament.

Counsel for Manitoba sought to distinguish this case on the ground that the *Statute of Westminster* did not embrace Southern Rhodesia, a point to which the Privy Council adverted. The *Statute of Westminster* will be considered later in these reasons, but if it had been in force in Southern Rhodesia it would be only under its terms and not through any conventional rule per se that the Parliament of the United Kingdom would have desisted from legislating for Southern Rhodesia.

Quite a number of cases were cited on which counsel for Manitobe relied to support his contention of conventions crystallizing into law. The chief support put forward for the "crystallization into law" proposition was the opinion of Duff C.J.C. in *Reference re Weekly Rest in Industrial Undertakings Act*, (1936) S.C.R. 461, better known as the *Labour Conventions* case when appealed to the Privy Council, (1937) A.C. 326, which took a different view on the constitutional merits than did the equally divided Supreme Court of Canada. The issue, so far as it touched the matter under discussion here, concerned the alleged want of power of the Governor General in Council, the federal executive, to enter into a treaty or accept an international obligation toward and with a foreign state, especially where the substance of the treaty or obligation related to matters which, legislatively within Canada, were within exclusive provincial competence.

The following portion of the reasons of Sir Lyman Duff contains the passage relied on, but extends it for more accurate context (at pp. 476-8):

With reference to the Report of the Conference of 1926, which in explicit terms recognizes treaties in the form of agreements between governments (to which His Majesty is not, in form, a party), it is said that since an Imperial Conference possesses no legislative power, its declarations do not operate to effect changes in the law, and it is emphatically affirmed that, in point of strict law, neither the Governor General nor any other Canadian authority has received from the Crown power to exercise the prerogative.

The argument is founded on the distinction it draws between constitutional convention and legal rule; and it is necessary to examine the contention that, in point of legal rule, as distinct from constitutional convention, the Governor General in Council had no authority to become party by ratification to the convention with which we are concerned.

There are various points of view from which this contention may be considered. First of all, constitutional law consists very largely of established constitutional usages recognized by the Courts as embodying a rule of law. An Imperial Conference, it is true, possesses no legislative authority. But there could hardly be more authoritative evidence as to constitutional usage than the declarations of such a Conference. The Conference of 1926 categorically recognizes treaties in the form of agreements between governments in which His Majesty does not formally appear, and in respect of which there has been no Royal intervention. It is the practice of the Dominion to conclude with foreign countries agreements in such form, and agreements even of a still more informal character — merely by an exchange of notes. Conventions under the auspices of the Labour Organization of the League of Nations invariably are ratified by the Government of the Dominion concerned. As a rule, the crystallization of constitutional usage into a rule of constitutional law to which the Courts will give effect is a slow process extending over a long period of time; but the Great War accelerated the pace of development in the region with which we are concerned, and it would seem that the usages to which I have referred, the practice, that is to say, under which Great Britain and the Dominions enter into agreements with foreign countries in the form of agreements between governments and of a still more informal character, must be recognized by the Courts as having the force of law.

Indeed, agreements between the Government of Canada and other governments in the form of an agreement between Governments, to which His Majesty is not a party, have been recognized by the Judicial Committee of the Privy Council as adequate in international law to create an international obligation binding upon Canada *Radio* Reference, (1932) A.C. 304) . . .

Ratification was the effective act which gave binding force to the convention. It was, as respects Canada, the act of the Government of Canada alone, and the decision mentioned appears, therefore, to negative decisively the contention that, in point of strict law, the Government of Canada is incompetent to enter into an international engagement.

What the learned Chief Justice was dealing with was an evolution which is characteristic of customary international law; the attainment by the Canadian federal executive of full and independent power to enter into international agreements. (Indeed, in speaking of "convention" in the last quoted paragraph, he was referring to an international agreement and, similarly, in the use of the word in the second last line of the second paragraph of the quotation and again in the middle of the third paragraph.) International law perforce has had to develop, if it was to exist at all, through commonly recognized political practices of states, there being no governing constitution, no legislating authority, no executive enforcement authority and no generally accepted judicial organ through which international law could be developed. The situation is entirely different in domestic law, in the position of a state having its own governing legislative, executive and judicial organs and, in most cases, an overarching written constitution.

Chief Justice Duff indicated his view of convention as allegedly maturing into law in a domestic setting in *Reference re Disallowance and Reservation of Provincial Legislation* , (1938) S.C.R. 71. There it was urged that a certain portion of s. 90 of the *British North America Act* (incorporating, in respect of the Provinces, ss. 56 and 57, with some modification) had by reason of convention become spent and was suspended by the alleged convention. As to this, the Chief Justice said (at p. 78):

> We are not concerned with constitutional usage. We are concerned with questions of law which, we repeat, must be determined by reference to the enactments of the *British North America Acts* of 1867 to 1930, the *Statute of Westminster* , and, it might be, to relevant statutes of the Parliament of Canada is there were any.
> Section 90 which, with the changes therein specified, re-enacts sections 55, 56 and 57 of the *B.N.A. Act* , is still subsisting. It has not been repealed or amended by the Imperial Parliament and it is quite clear that, by force of subsection 1 of section 7 of the *Statute of Westminster* , the Dominion Parliament did not acquire by that statute, any authority to repeal, amend or alter the *British North America Acts* . Whether or not, by force of section 91 (29) and section 91 (1) of the *B.N.A. Act* , the Dominion Parliament has authority to legislate in respect of reservation, it is not necessary to consider because no such legislation has been passed.
> The powers are, therefore, subsisting. Are they subject to any limitation or restriction?
> Once more, we are not concerned with constitutional usage or constitutional practice.

There is nothing in the other judgments delivered in the *Labour Conventions* case, either in the Supreme Court or in the Privy Council that takes the matter there beyond its international law setting or lends credence to the crystallization proposition urged by counsel for the Attorney General of Manitoba and, it should be said, supported by other Provinces and by observations in the reasons of the Newfoundland Court of Appeal. Other cases cited for the proposition turn out, on examination, to be instances where the Courts proceeded on firm statutory or other legal principles. This is as true of the observation of Viscount Sankey on the position of the Privy Council in *British Coal Corp. v. The King* , (1935) A.C. 500 at p. 510, as it is of the denial of injunctive relief in respect of disclosure of the Crossman diaries in *Attorney-General v. Jonathon Cape Ltd.* , (1976) 1 Q.B. 752. The Court pointed out in the latter case that it had the power to restrain breaches of confidence where demanded in the public interest, although the confidence stemmed from a convention respecting Cabinet deliberations. However, the need for restraint had gone because of the passage of time. The Court was applying its own legal principles as it might to any question of confidence, however it arose.

A close look at some other cases and issues raised on so-called crystallization reveals no support for the contention. Nothing need be said about Crown immunity or Crown prerogative, which rested firmly on common law principles and have long since been transformed by various statutes. Among cases put forward, were *Commercial Cable Co. v. Government of Newfoundland* , (1916) 2 A.C. 610, *Alexander E. Hull & Co. v. McKenna* , (1926) 1 R. 402 and *Copyright Owners v. E.M.I. (Australia) Pty. Ltd. (1958)* , 100 C.L.R. 597, *Blackburn v. Attorney-General* , (1971) 2 All E.R. 1380 and the judgment of this Court in the Senate Reference, *Re Authority of Parliament in relation to the Upper House* , (1980) 1 S.C.R. 54.

In the *Commercial Cable Co.* case, a certain contract was held not to be binding on the Government of Newfoundland when it was not approved by a resolution of the House of Assembly as required by a rule of the House promulgated pursuant to statute. *Hull v. McKenna* was the first instance of an application for leave to appeal to the Privy Council from the Court of Appeal, the final Court of the Irish Free

19

State, which had been recognized as a Dominion under a treaty with the United Kingdom. The question at issue was the application of Privy Council practice on petitions to it for leave to appeal. The legal issue, on which the case turned, was the manner in which the Privy Council exercised its discretion on such petitions.

The *Copyright Owners* case, somewhat involved in its facts, concerned the effect upon and in Australia of a British Act of 1928 and a subsequent Act of 1956. The latter Act repealed the *British Copyright Act* of 1911 which, pursuant to its terms had been brought into force in Australia by Commonwealth legislation. The British *Act* of 1911 expressly declared that it would not extend to a self-governing Dominion unless declared by the legislature of that Dominion to be in force there, and with certain limited modifications if thought desirable. The 1956 *Act*, as a post*Statute of Westminster Act* did not apply to Australia when there was no declaration that the Commonwealth had requested and consented to its application. Hence the 1911 British*Act* was left in force in Australia; indeed, it was so protected under the 1956 British *Act*, although as Dixon C.J. noted, it was perhaps unnecessary to say so in view of s. 4 of the*Statute of Westminster*.

The real issue concerned the British*Act* of 1928 which confirmed a Board of Trade order, resulting in the increase of the royalty payable for reproduction of musical works beyond that fixed by the *Act* of 1911. There was provision in the 1911 Act for alteration of rates through an inquiry by the Board of Trade and the making of an order to be confirmed by statute.

Although the *Statute of Westminster* was three years away, the High Court applied a rule of construction against any British legislative intention, even in 1928, to apply its legislation to Australia when it did not expressly say so. True, this took account of political practice but it was the Court's application of rules of interpretation which governed and the political practice would have counted for nothing if the British legislation of 1928 had been made expressly applicable to Australia. The following passage from the reasons of McTiernan J. is instructive (at p. 613):

. . .The rule of construction which found its source in the political and constitutional relations between the United Kingdom and the Commonwealth of Australia before the *Statute of Westminster* would raise a presumption that the Act of 1928 was not intended to operate of its own force in this country. Needless to say, it is a rule of construction which this Court would be expected to apply. The fact that the Parliament of the Commonwealth in adopting the *Copyright Act* 1911 (Imp.) made no special modifications in relation to s. 19 (3) does not seem to me to afford any reason for our departing from that rule of construction by holding that the Act of 1928 has force and effect in the Commonwealth. I think that it would be fanciful to say that although the latter Act does not apply in Australia as a piece of Imperial legislation, nevertheless, it may operate as no more than a fulfilment of the conditions prescribed by s. 19 (3) for altering the rates for the calculations of royalties. . . .

An *obiter* of Lord Denning in the Blackburn case was urged before the Court to support the crystallization contention. The case itself arose through an attempt to stall negotiations for entry by the United Kingdom into the European Common Market on the ground that it would involve the surrender by the British Parliament of some at least of its traditional sovereignty. All three Judges in the case agreed that there was no doubt of the power of the United Kingdom executive to enter into treaties and that this was beyond judicial control. Lord Denning's *obiter* was as follows (at p. 1382):

We have all been brought up to believe that, in legal theory, one Parliament cannot bind another and that no Act is irreversible. But legal theory does not always march alongside political reality. Take the *Statute of Westminster* 1931, which takes away the power of Parliament to legislate for the dominions. Can anyone imagine that Parliament could or would reverse that statute? Take the Acts which have granted independence to the dominions and territories overseas. Can anyone imagine that Parliament could or would reverse those laws and take away their independence? Most clearly not. Freedom once given cannot be taken away. Legal theory must give way to practical politics. . . .

What are the realities here? If Her Majesty's Ministers sign this treaty and Parliament enacts provisions to implement it, I do not envisage that Parliament would afterwards go back on it and try to withdraw from it. But, if Parliament should do so, then I say we will consider that event when it happens. We will then say whether Parliament can lawfully do it or not.

Both sides referred us to the valuable article by Professor H W R Wade in the Cambridge Law Journal in which he said that 'sovereignty is a political fact for which no purely legal authority can be constituted.' That is true. We must wait to see what happens before we pronounce on sovereignty in the Common Market.

The relevance of this to the legal issues in the case is not clear. Certainly the other two Judges who sat in the case, Salmon and Stamp L.JJ., were of the view that the only concern of the Court is with the interpretation of legislation when enacted, not with the Crown's conduct in entering into treaties.

Finally, there was an appeal to the Senate Reference decision of this Court. It is baffling how it can be said that this Court recognized convention as having *per se* grown into law. What was involved was a proposed federal enactment sought to be justified mainly under s. 91(1) of the *British North America Act*. This Court held that the proposal, at least in its main features, was beyond federal competence. Although the Court referred to certain historical background for perspective on the position of the Senate as it was dealt with under the *British North America Act*, its fundamental duty was to examine the validity of a proposed federal measure sought to be justified under a grant of federal power under the *Act*.

As to all the cases cited, it must be said that there is no independent force to be found in selective quotations from a portion of the reasons unless regard is had to issues raised and the context in which the quotations are found.

We were invited to consider academic writings on the matter under discussion. There is no consensus among the author-scholars, but the better and prevailing view is that expressed in an article by *Munro*, Laws and Conventions Distinguished (1975), 91 Law Q. rev. 218 where he says (at p. 228):

> The validity of conventions cannot be the subject of proceedings in a court of law. Reparation for breach of such rules will not be effected by any legal sanction. There are no cases which contradict these propositions. In fact, the idea of a court enforcing a mere convention is so strange that the question hardly arises.

Another passage from this article deserves mention, as follows (at p. 224):

> If in fact laws and conventions are different in kind, as is my argument, then an accurate and meaningful picture of the constitution may only be obtained if this distinction is made. If the distinction is blurred, analysis of the constitution is less complete; this is not only dangerous for the lawyer, but less than helpful to the political scientist. . . .

There is no difference in approach whether the issue arises in a unitary state or in a federal state: see Hogg, Constitutional Law of Canada (1977), at pp. 7-11.

A contrary view relied on by the provincial appellants is that expressed by Professor W.R. Lederman in two published articles, one entitled Process of Constitutional Amendment in Canada (1967), 12 McGill L.J. 371 and the second entitled Constitutional Amendment and Canadian Unity, (1978) Law Soc. U.C. Lectures, 17. As a respected scholar, Professor Lederman's views deserve more than cursory consideration. He himself recognized that there are contrary views, including those of an equally distinguished scholar, Profesor F.R. Scott: see *Scott*, Essays on the Constitution (1977), p. 144, 169, 204-205, 245, 370-371, 402. There is also the contrary view of Professor Hogg, already cited.

Professor Lederman relies in part on a line of cases that has already been considered, especially the reasons of Sir Lyman Duff in the *Labour Conventions* case. The leap from convention to law is explained almost as if there was a common law of constitutional law, but originating in political practice. That is simply not so. What is desirable as a political limitation does not translate into a legal limitation, without expression in imperative constitutional text or statute. The position advocated is all the more unacceptable when substantial provincial compliance or consent is by him said to be sufficient. Although Professor Lederman would not give a veto to Prince Edward Island, he would to Ontario or Quebec or British Columbia or Alberta. This is an impossible position for a Court to manage. Further reference to this is made later in these reasons.

VIII

Turning now to the authority or power of the two federal Houses to proceed by Resolution to forward the address and appended draft statutes to Her Majesty the Queen for enactment by the Parliament of the United Kingdom. There is no limit anywhere in law, either in Canada or in the United Kingdom (having regard to s. 18 of the *British North America Act*, as enacted by 1875 (U.K.), c. 38, which ties the privileges, immunities and powers of the federal Houses to those of the British House of Commons) to the power of the Houses to pass resolutions. Under s. 18 aforesaid, the federal Parliament may by statute define those privileges, immunities and powers, so long as they do not exceed those held and enjoyed by the British House of Commons at the time of the passing of the federal statute.

May, treatise on the Law, Privileges, Proceedings and Usages of Parliament (1976, 19th ed), a leading treatise on British parliamentary proceedings, states (at p. 382):

> Every question, when agreed to, assumes the form either of an order or of a resolution of the House. One or the other of these terms is applied in the records of the House to every motion which has been agreed to, and the application of the term is carefully regulated with reference to the content of the motion. By its orders the House directs its committees, its members, its officers, the order of its own proceedings and the acts of all persons whom they concern; by its resolutions the House declared its own opinions and purposes. . . .

This passage is repeated almost verbatim in *Beauchesne's* Parliamentary Rules and Forms (1978, 5th ed.), at p. 150. The *Senate and House of Commons Act*, R.S.C. 1970; c. S-8, ss. 4 and 5, reinforces what is set out in s. 18 of the *British North America Act*, as amended in 1875.

How Houses of Parliament proceed, how a provincial Legislative Assembly proceeds is in either case a matter of self-definition, subject to any overriding constitutional or self-imposed statutory or indoor prescription. It is unnecessary here to embark on any historical review of the "court" aspect of Parliament and the immunity of its procedures from judicial review. Courts come into the picture when legislation is enacted and not before (unless references are made to them for their opinion on a Bill or a proposed enactment). It would be incompatible with the self-regulating — "inherent" is as apt a word — authority of Houses of Parliament to deny their capacity to pass any kind of Resolution. Reference may appropriately be made to article 9 of the *Bill of Rights* of 1689, undoubtedly in force as part of the law of Canada, which provides that "proceedings in Parliament ought not to be impeached or questioned in any Court or place out of Parliament."

It is said, however, that where the Resolution touches provincial powers, as the one in question here does, there is a limitation on federal authority to pass it on to Her Majesty The Queen unless there is provincial consent. If there is such a limitation, it arises not from any limitation on the power to adopt Resolutions but from an external limitation based on other considerations which will shortly be considered.

Although the *British North America Act* itself is silent on the question of the power of the federal Houses to proceed by Resolution to procure an amendment to the Act by an address to Her Majesty, its silence gives positive support as much as it may reflect the negative. Quebec question B suggests in its formulation that there is the necessity of affirmative proof of the power asserted, but it would be equally consistent with constitutional precedent to require disproof. Moreover, if the two federal Houses had the power to proceed by Resolution, how is it that they have lost it?

For the moment, it is relevant to point out that even in those cases where an amendment to the *British North America Act* was founded on a Resolution of the federal Houses after having received provincial consent, there is no instance, save in the *British North America Act 1930* where such consent was recited in the Resolution. The matter remained, in short, a conventional one within Canada, without effect on the validity of the Resolution in respect of United Kingdom action. The point is underscored in relation to the very first amendment directly affecting provincial legislative power, that in 1940 which added "Unemployment Insurance" to the catalogue of exclusive federal powers. Sir William Jowitt, then Solicitor-General, and later Lord Chancellor, was asked in the British House of Commons about provincial consent when the amendment was in course of passage. The question put to him and his answer are as follows (see 362 U.K. Parl. Deb. 5th Series, H.C. 1177-1181);

Mr. Mander . . . In this bill we are concerned only with the Parliament of Canada, but, as a matter of interest, I would be obliged if the Solicitor-General would say whether the Provincial Canadian Parliaments are in agreement with the proposals submitted by the Dominion Parliament . . .

Sir William Jowitt . . . One might think that the Canadian Parliament was in some way subservient to ours, which is not the fact. The true position is that at the request of Canada this old machinery still survives until something better is thought of, but we square the legal with the constitutional position by passing these Acts only in the form that the Canadian Parliament require and at the request of the Canadian Parliament.

My justification to the House for this Bill — and it is important to observe this — is not on the merits of the proposal, which is a matter for the Canadian Parliament; if we were to embark upon that, we might trespass on what I conceive justification for this enactment is that we are doing in this way what the Parliament of Canada desires to do . . .

In reply to the hon. Member for East Wolverhampton (Mr. Mander), I do not know what the view of the Provincial Parliaments is. I know, however, that when the matter was before the Privy Council some of the Provincial Parliaments supported the Dominion Parliament. It is a sufficient justification for the Bill that we are morally bound to act on the ground that we have here the request of the Dominion Parliament and that we must operate the old machinery which has been left over at their request in accordance with their wishes.

IX

This Court is being asked, in effect, to enshrine as a legal imperative a principle of unanimity for constitutional amendment to overcome the anomaly — more of an anomaly today than it was in 1867 — that the *British North America Act* contained no provision for effecting amendments by Canadian action alone. Although Saskatchewan has, alone of the eight Provinces opposing the federal package embodied in the Resolution, taken a less stringent position, eschewing unanimity but without quantifying the substantial support that it advocates, the Provinces, parties to the References and to the appeals here, are entitled to have this Court's primary consideration of their views.

The effect of those views, if they are correct in their legal position, is, of course, to leave at least the formal amending authority in the United Kingdom Parliament. Reference will be made later to the ingredients of the arguments on legality. The effect of the present Resolution is to terminate any need to resort to the United Kingdom Parliament in the future. In line with its rejection of unanimity, Saskatchewan asserted that it sees no violation of the principles of federalism in the Resolution so far as concerns the amending formula proposed thereby.

An important question was raised by the Saskatchewan position which invited this Court to take a severable view of the substance of the Resolution, namely, to hive off the *Charter of Rights and Freedoms* and perhaps other elements, save the amending formula and the patriation feature. This was not the position of the Attorney General of Canada nor of any of the other provincial Attorneys General; they were all of the view that it was the whole package that was involved in the legal issue posed by question 3 and question B. Indeed, the legal arguments pro and con do not engage the contents of the package, and it is impossible to qualify the issue of legality by considerations of fairness or equity or political acceptability or even judicial desirability.

The stark legal question is whether this Court can enact by what would be judicial legislation a formula of unanimity to initiate the amending process which would be binding not only in Canada but also on the Parliament of the United Kingdom with which amending authority would still remain. It would be anomalous indeed, overshadowing the anomaly of a Constitution which contains no provision for its amendment, for this Court to say retroactively that in law we have had an amending formula all along, even if we have not hitherto known it; or, to say, that we have had in law one amending formula, say from 1867 to 1931, and a second amending formula that has emerged after 1931. No one can gainsay the desirability of federal-provincial accord of acceptable compromise. That does not, however, go to legality. As Sir William Jowitt said, and quoted earlier, we must operate the old machinery perhaps one more time.

X

The provincial contentions asserted a legal incapacity in the federal Houses to proceed with the Resolution which is the subject of the References and of the appeals here. Joined to this assertion was a claim that the United Kingdom Parliament had, in effect, relinquished its legal power to act on a Resolution such as the one before this Court, and that it could only act in relation to Canada if a request was made by "the proper authorities." The federal Houses would be such authorities if provincial powers or interests would not be affected; if they would be, then the proper authorities would include the Provinces. It is not that the Provinces must be joined in the federal address to Her Majesty the Queen; that was not argued. Rather their consent (or, as in the Saskatchewan submission, substantial provincial compliance or approval) was required as a condition of the validity of the process by address and resolution and, equally, as a condition of valid action thereon by the United Kingdom Parliament.

There are a number of interwoven strands in this posi-

27

tion which must be separated for proper analysis and assessment. They include some dependence on the *Balfour Declaration* arising out of the Imperial Conference of 1926, and also on the Imperial Conference of 1930, the last-mentioned Conference preceded by a meeting of experts in 1929 on the Operation of Dominion Legislation. Then there is a considerable emphasis on a particular view of the *Statute of Westminster* in respect of some of its terms, and especially ss. 4 and 7(1). Perhaps most important is a conjoint contention based on sovereignty (softened in reply by the Attorney General of Manitoba) and on what are said to be basic presuppositions and constitutional underpinnings of Canadian federalism.

XI

The Court was invited to regard the *Balfour Declaration* of 1926 as embracing the Provinces of Canada (and, presumably, the states of the sister Dominion of Australia) in its reference to "autonomous communities." That well-known statement of principle, a political statement in the context of evolving independence of the Dominions in their relations with the United Kingdom, is as follows:

They are autonomous Communities within the British Empire, equal in status, in no way subordinate one to another in any aspect of their domestic or external affairs, though united by a common allegiance to the Crown, and freely associated as members of the British Commonwealth of Nations.

It is impossible to seek nourishment for the provincial position in these appeals in this Declaration. The Provinces did not come into the picture in the march to the *Statute of Westminster, 1931* until after the 1929 Conference on the Operation of Dominion Legislation, although to a degree before the Imperial Conference of 1930. They then made their views known on certain aspects of the looming statute, views which were canvassed in a Dominion-Provincial Conference in 1931. The main concern touched the proposed repeal of the *Colonial Laws Validity Act (U.K.)*, c. 63 and the effect that this might have on the amendment of the *British North America Act*, a matter to be considered later in these reasons.

Although the *Balfour Declaration* cannot, of itself, support the assertion of provincial autonomy in the wide sense contended for, it seems to have been regarded as retroactively having that effect by reason of the ultimate enactment of the *Statute of Westminster*. That statute is put forward not only as signifying an equality of status as between the Dominion and the Provinces *vis-a-vis* the United Kingdom Parliament, but also as attenuating the theretofore untrammelled legislative authority of that Parliament in relation to Canada where provincial interests are involved. The germ of these consequences was said by the Newfoundland Court of Appeal to be in the *Balfour Declaration*, arising out of the Imperial Conference of 1926 and embodied in the Report of that Conference.

The following summarizing passage on question 3 is contained in the reasons of the Newfoundland Court of Appeal:

In our opinion, the constitutional status of the Provinces of Canada as autonomous communities was confirmed and perfected by (a) the Statute of Westminster giving effect to the constitutional principle declared by the Imperial Conference that both the United Kingdom and the Dominions are autonomous communities equal in status, in no way subordinate one to another in any aspect of their domestic or external affairs; (b) the recognition by that Conference of the division of power among the constituent parts that make up the Dominion of Canada by which each is autonomous, in no way subordinate one to another; and, (c) the surrender by the Imperial Parliament to the Provinces of its legislative sovereignty, over matters declared by the British North America Act to be within the exclusive legislative competence of the Provinces. The modification of that constitutional status was thereby withdrawn from future British parliamentary competence except with the consent of the Provinces.

While the Parliament of Great Britain, in the absence of notice to the contrary, is constitutionally entitled to accept a Resolution passed by both Houses of the Canadian Parliament as a proper request for a constitutional amendment from the whole Canadian community, it is nonetheless precluded, for the reasons stated above, from enacting an amendment restricting the powers, rights and privileges granted the Provinces by the British North America Act, and enlarged by the Statute of Westminister over the objections of the Provinces.

If the significance attached to the *Statute of Westminster* is, indeed, what is asserted in the above-quoted passage and what has been urged by the Provinces in this Court, there is no need to resort to the *Balfour Declaration*, save possibly as a footnote. The course of events leading to the *Statute of Westminster* is detailed in numerous writings. It is sufficient to refer, in general, to the discussion in *Wheare*, the Statute of Westminster and Dominion Status (1953, 5th ed.), *passim;* and see, especially, Chapter VII, The Statute and the Legal Status of Canada.

The submissions made on the *Statute of Westminster* by counsel who were before this Court engage (1) the preamble to the *Statute;* (2) s. 2(1)(2); (3) s. 3; (4) s. 4 and (5) s. 7(1)(2)(3). These provisions are in the following terms:

WHEREAS the delegates of His Majesty's Governments in the United Kingdom, the Dominion of Canada, the Commonwealth of Australia, the Dominion of New Zealand, the Union of South Africa, the Irish Free State and Newfoundland, at Imperial Conferences holden at Westminster in the years of our Lord nineteen hundred and twenty-six and nineteen hundred and thirty did concur in making the declarations and resolutions set forth in the Reports of the said Conferences:

And whereas it is meet and proper to set out by way of preamble to this Act that, inasmuch as the Crown is the symbol of the free association of the members of the British Commonwealth of Nations, and as they are united by a common allegiance to the Crown, it would be in accord with the established constitutional position of all the members of the Commonwealth in relation to one another that any alteration in the law touching the Succession to the Throne or the Royal Style and Titles shall hereafter require the assent as well of the Parliaments of all the Dominions as of the Parliament of the United Kingdom.

And whereas it is in accord with the established constitutional position that no law hereafter made by the Parliament of the United Kingdom shall extend to any of the said Dominions as part of the law of that Dominion otherwise than at the request and with the consent of that Dominion:

And whereas it is necessary for the ratifying, confirming and establishing of certain of the said declarations and resolutions of the said Conferences that a law be made and enacted in due form by authority of the Parliament of the United Kingdom:

And whereas the Dominion of Canada, the Commonwealth of Australia, the Dominion of New Zealand, the Union of South Africa, the Irish Free State and Newfoundland have severally requested and consented to the submission of a measure to the Parliament of the United Kingdom for making such provision with regard to the matters aforesaid as is hereafter in this Act contained:

Now, therefore, be it enacted by the King's most Excellent Majesty by and with the advice and consent of the Lords Spiritual and Temporal, and Commons, in this present Parliament assembled, and by the authority of the same, as follows: ——

2. —— (1) The Colonial Laws Validity Act, 1865, shall not apply to any law made after the commencement of this Act by the Parliament of a Dominion.

(2) No law and no provision of any law made after the commencement of this Act by the Parliament of a Dominion shall be void or inoperative on the ground that it is repugnant to the law of England, or to the provisions of any existing or future Act of Parliament of the United Kingdom, or to any order, rule or regulation made under any such Act, and the powers of the Parliament of a Dominion shall include the power to repeal or amend any such Act, order, rule or regulation in so far as the same is part of the law of the Dominion.

3. It is hereby declared and enacted that the Parliament of a Dominion has full power to make laws having extra-territorial operation.

4. No Act of Parliament of the United Kingdom passed after the commencement of this Act shall extend, or be deemed to extend, to a Dominion as part of the law of that Dominion, unless it is expressly declared in that Act that that Dominion has requested, and consented to. the enactment thereof.

7. —— (1) Nothing in this Act shall be deemed to apply to the repeal,

amendment or alteration of the British North America Acts, 1867 to 1930, or any order, rule or regulation made thereunder.

(2) The provisions of section two of this Act shall extend to laws made by any of the Provinces of Canada and to the powers of the legislatures of such Provinces.

(3) The powers conferred by this Act upon the Parliament of Canada or upon the legislatures of the Provinces shall be restricted to the enactment of laws in relation to matters within the competence of the Parliament of Canada or of any of the legislatures of the Provinces respectively.

There is nothing in the preamble that relates to the Provinces other than the reference to the Report of the Imperial Conference of 1930. What emerged prior to this Conference was an understandable provincial concern that the effect of the proposed repeal of the *Colonial Laws Validity Act* in favour of the Parliament of a Dominion and, in addition, the effect of what became s. 2(2) of the *Statute* might enlarge federal power to alter, by its own legislation, provisions of the *British North America Act.* Thus it was that the Conference of 1930 placed on record (Cmd. 3717, pp. 17-18):

> that the sections of the Statute relating to the Colonial Laws Validity Act should be so drafted as not to extend to Canada unless the Statute was enacted in response to such requests as are appropriate to an amendment of the British North America Act. It is also seemed desirable to place on record the view that the sections should not subsequently be extended to Canada except by an Act of the Parliament of the United Kingdom enacted in response to such requests as are appropriate to an amendment of the British North America Act.

The *Colonial Laws Validity Act* was intended to be a liberating statute, releasing colonial legislatures from subservience to British common law (subject to Privy Council authority) and from subservience of British statute law unless such statute law applied expressly or by necessary implication to the colony. In the evolution of independence of the Dominions, it came to be recognized tha the United Kingdom should no longer legislate at its own instance for any Dominion; and that the latter should be free to repeal any British legislation that was or would be made applicable to it. Hence, the statement in the preamble and hence ss. 2 and 4 in their application to a Dominion. Following the Imperial Conference of 1930 and as a result of the Dominion-Provincial Conference of 1931, the Provinces obtained an assurance that they too would benefit by the repeal of the *Colonial Laws Validity Act* and by being empowered to repeal

31

any British legislation made applicable to them. This was achieved by s. 7(2) of the *Statute of Westminster.* There did not appear to be any need to include them in s. 4.

The most important issue was, however, the position of the Dominion *vis-a-vis* the *British North America Act.* What s. 7(1), reinforced by s. 7(3), appeared to do was to maintain the *status quo ante;* that is, to leave any changes in the *British North America Act* (that is, such changes which, under its terms, could not be carried out by legislation of the Provinces or of the Dominion) to the prevailing situation, namely, with the legislative authority of the United Kingdom Parliament being left untouched. As Sir William Jowitt put it, in the passage quoted earlier (in connection with the debate on the unemployment insurance amendment), "the old machinery" remained in place as a result of the *Statute of Westminster.* No other conclusion is supportable on any fair reading of the terms of the *Statute of Westminster.*

The Provinces, other than Ontario and New Brunswick, do not agree with this view of the *Statue of Westminster.* There were a number of positions taken by them. Much was made, especially in the submissions of counsel for the Attorney General of Manitoba, of the use of the plural in the phrase "such requests as are appropriate to an amendment of the British North America Act" in the passage above-quoted from the Report of the 1930 Imperial Conference. The point taken from this was said to be a re-emphasis of that portion of the 1929 Conference on the Operation of Dominion Legislation which, in referring to the *British North America Act,* said that the question of the proper method of amending it should remain "for future consideration by the appropriate Canadian authorities." It was contended, certainly with justification, that the "proper Canadian authorities" were the Dominion and the Provinces and, presumably, it would be for them to decide whether it would be the respective Governments or Parliament and the Legislatures, or both, and also what degree of agreement among the Provinces would be proper. It is, however, impossible to draw from this any legal rule of conduct because, ultimately, whatever political consensus might be achieved, there would still be the legal necessity of final United Kingdom legislative action.

The matter is not advanced by the follow-up Dominion-Provincial Conference of 1931. As the brief summary of the Conference stated, its purpose was,

> . . . to give the Provinces an opportunity to express their views with regard to the Statute of Westminster and the proposed Section, numbered 7, which will be inserted to deal exclusively with the Canadian position. No objection was made to the principle of the proposed legislation, and a proposal that the provisions of the Statute relating to the repeal of the Colonial Laws Validity Act should extend to the Provinces was approved. The Canadian Section (7) was drafted and found satisfactory by all the Provinces, though Quebec asked for further time for consideration. Meanwhile, the approval of the Quebec Government has been received.

The Conference summary continued as follows:

> Certain other constitutional questions arose during the Conference. *Some Provinces desired that the question of powers and procedure in respect to constitutional amendment should be discussed together with the wider subject of constitutional relations between Dominions (sic) and Provinces.* This was found to be impossible at that meeting, but it was agreed that a constitutional conference should be summoned as soon as possible. It was the general opinion that such a conference a method of amending the Canadian constitution by Canadian agencies might be discovered which would reconcile that two essential features of reasonable elasticity of change and the preservation of provincial rights.

The sentence (in italics) in the above-quoted Conference summary shows quite clearly that as of 1930, there was certainly no rule of law with respect to constitutional amendment. No change was effected in the legal position by the *Statute of Westminster.*

It was also urged upon this Court that s. 7(1), which in terms ("nothing in this Act shall be deemed to apply to . . . the British North America Acts, 1867 to 1930") removes the *British North America Act* (at least as it then stood) from the application of any terms of the *Statute of Westminster,* was addressed to ss. 2 and 3 and not to s. 4. The argument goes that s. 7(1) does not exclude the application of s. 4; that s. 4 must be read in its preclusive effect on a Dominion as having the Provinces in view; that the "request and consent" which must be declared in a British statute to make it applicable to Canada, is the request and consent of the Dominion and the Provinces if the statute is one affecting provincial interests or powers, for example, an amendment of the *British North America Act* as envisaged by the Resolution herein. The word "Dominion" in s. 4, it is said, must be read in what may be called a conjoint or collective sense as including both the Dominion and the Provinces; otherwise, it is submitted, the purpose of the *Statute of Westminster* would be defeated. A difference, said to be significant, is pointed up in the reference to "Parliament of a Dominion" in s. 3 and the bare word "Dominion" in s. 4.

Nothing in the language of the *Statute of Westminster* supports the provincial position yet it is on this interpretation that it is contended that the Parliament of the United Kingdom has relinquished or yielded its previous omnipotent legal authority in relation to the *British North America Act*, one of its own statutes. As an argument on question 3 and question B (in its legal aspect), it asserts a legal diminution of United Kingdom legislative supremacy. The short answer to this ramified submission is that it distorts both history and ordinary principles of statutory or constitutional interpretation. The plain fact is that s. 7(1) was enacted to obviate any inference of direct unilateral federal power to amend the *British North America Act* and that it is s. 7(3) that is addressed to s. 2 and not s. 7(1). It is for this reason that it was unnecessary to provide in respect of Canada what was provided by s. 9(3) in respect of Australia, namely, that in the application of the *Statute of Westminster* to the Commonwealth of Australia "the request and consent referred to in section 4 shall mean the request and consent of the Parliament and Government of the Commonwealth." There is, moreover, an interpretation section in the *Statute of Westminster*, being s. 1, and in it "Dominion" means any of the following Dominions, "that is to say the Dominion of Canada, the Commonwealth of Australia, the Dominion of New Zealand, the Union of South Africa, the Irish Free State and Newfoundland." The reference to "Parliament of a Dominion" in s. 3 and "Dominion" in s. 4 is easily explained by the context. The argument on the *Statute of Westminster* is untenable, but it leaves for more anxious consideration the effect of the removal of the *British North America Act* from the *Statute of Westminster* and the preservation by s. 7(3) of the existing distribution of legislative powers under the *British North America Act*.

34

XII

This leads to the submissions made on the sovereignty of the Provinces in respect of their powers under the *British North America Act*, the term "sovereignty" being modified in the course of argument to "supremacy." Allied to this was the contention that Canada cannot do indirectly what it cannot do directly; it could not by an enactment of its own accomplish that which is proposed by the Resolution. Such an enactment would be clearly *ultra vires* as to most of the provisions put forward by the Resolution, and it should not be able to improve its position in law by invoking the aid of the United Kingdom Parliament. Moreover, even if the Parliament of the United Kingdom retained its formal legal authority over the *British North America Act*, as one of its enactments, it was in the words used by the late and at the time, former Justice Rand, "a bare legislative trustee," subject as a matter of law to the direction of the beneficiaries, namely, the Dominion and the Provinces, in respect of the Resolution.

It will be convenient to deal at this point with the "direct-indirect" contention and with the notion of legislative trusteeship, before returning to the main submission on provincial legislative supremacy. That submission involves a consideration of the character of Canadian federalism and it must, of course, be carefully assessed.

The direct-indirect contention, taken by itself, amounts to this: that whether or not the federal Houses can seek to obtain enactment of the draft statute appended to the Resolution, it would, in any event, be illegal to invoke United Kingdom authority to do for Canada what it cannot do itself. The maxim "you cannot do indirectly what you cannot do directly" is a much abused one. It was used to invalidate provincial legislation in *Madden v. Nelson and Fort Sheppard Ry.* (1889) A.C. 626. It is a pithy way of describing colourable legislation: see *Ladore v. Bennett,* (1939) A.C. 468, at p. 482. However, it does not preclude a limited legislature from achieving directly under one head of legislative power what it could not do directly under another head. The question, of course, remains whether the two federal Houses may alone initiate and carry through the process to invoke the competence of the United Kingdom Parliament.

At least with regard to the amending formula the process in question here concerns not the amendment of a complete constitution but rather the completion of an incomplete constitution.

We are involved here with a finishing operation, with fitting a piece into the constitutional edifice; it is idle to expect to find anything in the *British North America Act* that regulates the process that has been initiated in this case. Were it otherwise, there would be no need to resort to the Resolution procedure invoked here, a procedure which takes account of the intergovernmental and international link between Canada and Great Britain. There is no comparable link that engaged the Provinces with Great Britain. Moreover, it is to confuse the issue of process, which is the basic question here, with the legal competence of the British Parliament when resort is had to the direct-indirect argument. The legal competence of that Parliament, for the reasons already given, remains unimpaired, and it is for it alone to determine if and how it will act.

The late Justice Rand used the words "a bare legislative trustee" in the Holmes Lecture delivered at Harvard Law School under the title "Some Aspects of Canadian Constitutionalism" and reproduced in (1960), 38 Can. Bar Rev. 135. His use of the phrase came in the course of his discussion of the effect of the *Statute of Westminster*. He said this (at p. 145):

> Legislatively, a unique situation has been created. The British Parliament has in effect become a bare legislative trustee for the Dominion; the constitutional organ for altering the provisions of the Canadian constitution contained in the Act of 1867 remains so far the British Parliament; but the political direction resides in the Parliament of the Dominion; the former has conceded its residue of legislative power vis-a-vis Canada, to be no more than means for effecting the will of Canada. It might happen, although it is most unlikely, that the British Parliament should demur to a request for a legislative amendment, as, for example, involving important legislative effects not concurred in by one or more of the provinces; but that amounts to no more than saying that the Canadian people would not yet have agreed on the mode of modifying their internal constitutional relations. Once that means has been agreed upon, legislative independence, not only in substance but in form, will have been attained.

The Newfoundland Court of Appeal adopted the phrase but decided that Justice Rand should not have limited the suggested trusteeship as being for the Dominion of Canada alone. Moreover, the Court overlooked a central point in the Rand lecture that "the political direction resides in the Parliament of the Dominion." Thus the Court said:

> We adopt that statement fully with the important addition that the Parliament of Great Britain is a 'bare legislative trustee' for *both* the Federal Parliament and the Provincial Legislatures in relation to the matters within their respective legislative competence. Any amendment enacted by the Parliament of Great Britain affecting the legislative competence of either of the parties, without that party's consent, would not only be contrary to the intendment of the Statute of Westminster, but it could defeat the whole scheme of the Canadian Federal constitution.

It is enough to counter this assessment of the Newfoundland Court of Appeal by referring to what Gerin-Lajoie said in his seminal text Constitutional Amendment in Canada (1950), at p. 138:

> While the Parliament of the United Kingdom is precluded from enacting any constitutional amendment without a proper request from Canada the only competent voice of Canada for this purpose is that of the federal power. The provincial authorities — either executive or legislative — have no *locus standi* to move the British Parliament or Government with a view to securing an amendment to the federal Constitution.

It is obvious that any change in the legislative power of either Parliament or the provincial legislatures would directly affect the other. The thrust of the Newfoundland Court of Appeal's remarks just quoted goes more properly to the submissions and contentions on the nature of Canadian federalism than to any intendment of the *Statute of Westminster*.

Whatever the statute may import as to intra-Canadian conventional procedures, there is nothing in it or in the proceedings leading up to it that casts any doubt in law as to the undiminished authority of the Parliament of the United Kingdom over the *British North America Act*.

XIII

At bottom, the challenge to the competency in law of the federal Houses to seek enactment by the Parliament of the United Kingdom of the statutes embodied in the Resolution is based on the recognized supremacy of provincial Legislatures in relation to the powers conferred upon them under the *British North America Act,* a supremacy *vis-a-vis* the federal Parliament. Reinforcement, or perhaps the foundation of this supremacy is said to lie in the nature or character of Canadian federalism.

The supremacy position, taken alone, needs no further justification than that found in the respective formulations of the powers of Parliament and the provincial Legislatures in ss. 91 and 92 of the *British North America Act.* Federal paramountcy is, however, the general rule in the actual exercise of these powers. This notwithstanding, the exclusiveness of the provincial powers (another way of expressing supremacy and more consonant with the terms of the *British North America Act*) cannot be gainsaid. The long list of judicial decisions, beginning with *Hodge v. The Queen* (1883), 9 App. Cas. 117 and carrying through such cases as *Liquidators of the Maritime Bank v. Receiver General of New Brunswick,* (1892) A.C. 437 and the *Labour Conventions* case where the Privy Council expressed its "watertight compartment view" of legislative power (see (1937) A.C. 326, at p. 354) provide adequate support for the principle of exclusiveness or supremacy but, of course, within the limits of the *British North America Act* .

Although there are what have been called unitary features in the *British North America Act* , involving overriding powers (to be distinguished from paramountcy of legislation) in the federal Parliament and Government, their modification of exclusive provincial authority does not detract from that authority to any substantial degree. Thus, the federal declaratory power under s. 92(10) (c) has a limited operation; reservation and disallowance of provincial legislation, although in law still open, have, to all intents and purposes, fallen into disuse. The fact of appointment of the Lieutenant-Governors of the Provinces by the central Government does not, as a practical matter, have any significance for provincial powers when, under the law, the Lieutenant-Governor is as much the personal representative of the Crown as is the Governor-General. In each case, the representation is, of course, in respect of the powers respectively assigned to Parliament and the Legislatures. Moreover, since there is an international, a foreign relations aspect involved in the relationship of Canada and Great Britain, any formal communication between a Province and its Lieutenant-Governor with the United Kingdom Government or with the Queen, must be through the federal Government or through the Governor-General.

It is important in this connection to emphasize that the Government of Canada had, by 1923, obtained recognition internationally of its independent power to enter into external obligations when it negotiated the Halibut Treaty with the United States. Great Britain understood this by that time as did the United States. The subsequent Imperial Conferences added confirmation, sanctified by the *Statute of Westminster* which also put internal independence from Great Britain on a legal foundation. The remaining badge of subservience, the need to resort to the British Parliament to amend the *British North America Act*, although preserved by the *Statute of Westminster*, did not carry any diminution of Canada's legal right in international law, and as a matter of Canadian constitutional law, to assert its independence in external relations, be they with Great Britain or other countries. The matter is emphasized by the judgment of this Court in *Reference re Offshore Mineral Rights*, (1967)f S.C.R. 792, at p. 816. This is a relevant consideration in the appeals which are before this Court.

What is put forward by the Provinces which oppose the forwarding of the address without provincial consent is that external relations with Great Britain in this respect must take account of the nature and character of Canadian federalism. It is contended that a legal underpinning of their position is to be found in the Canadian federal system as reflected in historical antecedents, in the pronouncements of leading political figures and in the preamble to the *British North America Act.*

The arguments from history do not lead to any consistent view or any single view of the nature of the *British North America Act;* selective interpretations are open and have been made; see Report of the Royal Commission on Dominion-Provincial Relations (1940), Book 1, pp. 29 ff. History cannot alter the fact that in law there is a British statute to construe and apply in relation to a matter, fundamental as it is, that is not provided for by the statute. Practices which took account of evolving Canadian independence, did, of course, develop. They had both intra-Canadian and extra-Canadian aspects in relation to British legislative authority. The former have already been canvassed, both in the reasons on question 2 and question B and, to a degree, in these reasons. Theories, whether of a full compact theory (which, even factually, cannot be sustained, having regard to federal power to create new Provinces out of federal territories, which was exercised in the creation of Alberta and Saskatchewan) or of a modified compact theory, as urged by some of the Provinces, operate in the political realm, in political science studies. They do not engage the law, save as they might have some peripheral relevance to actual provisions of the *British North America Act* and its interpretation and application. Thus it is, to take one example, that in the *Nova Scotia Interdelegation case, Attorney-General of Nova Scotia v. Attorney General of Canada,* (1951) S.C.R. 31, Rinfret C.J. said (at P. 34):

The constitution of Canada does not belong either to Parliament, or to the Legislatures; it belongs to the country and it is there that the citizens of the country will find the protection of the rights to which they are entitled. It is part of that protection that Parliament can legislate only on the subject matters referred to it by section 91 and that each Province can legislate exclusively on the subject matters referred to it by section 92.

This was said, however, in the context of an issue raised under the terms of the *British North America Act,* the issue being whether there could be interdelegation between the Parliament of Canada and the Provincial Legislatures of their respective legislative powers which, as to each level of authority, where conferred as exclusive powers. In the Court below, the Nova Scotia Supreme Court *en banc,* Chief Justice Chisholm remarked that the *British North America Act* is not a counter for the exchange of constitutional wares: see (1948) 4 D.L.R. 1, at p. 6.

The statement, above-quoted, of Chief Justice Rinfret carries no independent legal consequence; it simply underscores the imperative character of the distribution of legislative power. In short, as in the attempt to argue crystallization of convention into law, there is nothing in the reference to theories of federalism reflected in some case law that goes beyond their use as an aid to a justiciable question raised apart from them.

So too, with pronouncements by political figures or persons in other branches of public life. There is little profit in parading them.

Support for a legal requirement of provincial consent to the Resolution that is before this Court, consent which is also alleged to condition United Kingdom response to the Resolution, is, finally, asserted to lie in the preamble of the British North America Act itself, and in the reflection, in the substantive terms of the Act, of what are said to be fundamental presuppositions in the preamble as to the nature of Canadian federalism. The preamble recites (and the whole of it is reproduced) the following:

> WHEREAS the Provinces of Canada, Nova Scotia and New Brunswick have expressed their Desire to be federally united into One Dominion under the Crown of the United Kingdom of Great Britain and Ireland, with a Constitution similar in Principle to that of the United Kingdom:
> And whereas such a Union would conduce to the Welfare of the Provinces and promote the Interests of the British Empire:
> And whereas on the Establishment of the Union by Authority of Parliament it is expedient, not only that the Constitution of the Legislative Authority in the Dominion be provided for, but also that the Nature of the Executive Government therein be declared:
> And whereas it is expedient that Provision be made for the eventual Admission into the Union of other Parts of the *British North America Act:*

What is stressed is the desire of the named provinces "to be federally united . . . with a Constitution similar in principle to that of the United Kingdom." The preamble speaks also of union into "one Dominion" and of the establishment of the Union "by authority of Parliament," that is the United Kingdom Parliament. What, then, is to be drawn from the preamble as a matter of law? A preamble, needless to say, has no enacting force but, certainly, it can be called in aid to illuminate provisions of the statute in which it appears. Federal union "with a constitution similar in principle to that of the United Kingdom" may well embrace responsible government and some common law aspects of the United Kingdom's unitary constitutionalism, such as the rule of law and Crown prerogatives and immunities. The "rule of law" is a highly textured expression, importing many things which are beyond the need of these reasons to

41

explore but conveying, for example, a sense of orderliness, of subjection to known legal rules and of executive accountability to legal authority. Legislative changes may alter common law prescriptions, as has happened with respect to Crown prerogatives and immunities. There is also an internal contradiction in speaking of federalism in the light of the invariable principle of British parliamentary supremacy. Of course, the resolution of this contradiction lies in the scheme of distribution of legislative power, but this owes nothing to the preamble, resting rather on its own exposition in the substantive terms of the *British North America Act.*

There is not and cannot be any standardized federal system from which particular conclusions must necessarily be drawn. Reference was made earlier to what were called unitary features of Canadian federalism and they operate to distinguish Canadian federalism from that of Australia and that of the United States. Allocations of legislative power differ as do the institutional arrangements through which power is exercised. This Court is being asked by the Provinces which object to the so-called federal "package" to say that the internal distribution of legislative power must be projected externally, as a matter of law, although there is no legal warrant for this assertion and, indeed, what legal authority exists (as in s. 3 of the *Statute of Westminster*) denies this provincial position.

At bottom, it is this distribution, it is the allocation of legislative power as between the central Parliament and the provincial Legislatures that the Provinces rely on as precluding unilateral federal action to seek amendments to the *British North America Act* that affect, whether by limitation or extension, provincial legislative authority. The Attorney General of Canada was pushed to the extreme by being forced to answer affirmatively the theoretical question whether in law the federal Government could procure an amendment to the *British North America Act* that would turn Canada into a unitary state. That is not what the present Resolution envisages because the essential federal character of the country is preserved under the enactments proposed by the Resolution.

That, it is argued, is no reason for conceding unilateral federal authority to accomplish, through invocation of legislation by the United Kingdom Parliament, the purposes of the Resolution. There is here, however, an unprecedented situation in which the one constant since the enactment of the *British North America Act* in 1867 has been the legal authority of the United Kingdom Parliament to amend it. The law knows nothing of any requirement of provincial consent, either to a resolution of the federal Houses or as a condition of the exercise of United Kingdom legislative power.

In the result, the third question in the Manitoba and Newfoundland cases should, as a matter of law, be answered in the negative and question B should, in its legal aspect, be answered in the affirmative.

XIV

There remains for consideration question 4 in the Newfoundland Reference. The question, in effect, asks if the matters therein raised could happen under the amending formula in the draft statute appended to the Resolution proposed for adoption by the two federal Houses. There were, as previously noted, some changes in the draft statute prior to its adoption by the federal Houses and a change as well in the numbering of some of the sections relevant to question 4. However, it is unnecessary to go into these number changes because the Attorney General of Canada agrees with the conclusions of the Newfoundland Court of Appeal as set out in the first three parts of its answer to the question, and the Attorney General of Newfoundland agrees with the Attorney General of Canada that the Newfoundland Court of Appeal was in error in the fourth part of its answer to the question. It was wrong to say that in a referendum under s. 42 (as it then was) of the proposed statute (now s. 46) the approval of the majority of the people in each Province was required. The proper view was that only the approval of the majority of the people voting in a referendum in those Provinces; the approval of whose Legislatures would be required under the general amending formula, would be necessary.

The Attorney General of Canada agreed with the Newfoundland Court of Appeal that an unqualified answer to question 4 might be misleading and he submitted what he considered to be better answers to question 4. Since there was substantial agreement before this Court by the Attorney General of Canada and the Attorney General of Newfoundland as to the proper answer to question 4, it is unnecessary to dwell on its details here. Moreover, it involves an assessment of the substantive terms of the draft statute proposed for enactment by the United Kingdom Parliament, and, in that respect, it is an example of the specifics which were sought in the answer to question 1 and which, it was agreed by counsel, need not be elaborated. It is hence unnecessary to say more on question 4, in the recognition also that this Court is not concerned here with the wisdom of the proposed enactment.

XV

Nothing said in these reasons is to be construed as either favouring or disapproving the proposed amending formula or the *Charter of Rights and Freedoms* or any of the other provisions of which enactment is sought. the questions put to this Court do not ask for its approval or disapproval of the contents of the so-called "package".

What is central here is the untrammelled authority at law of the two federal Houses to proceed as they wish in the management of their own procedures and hence to adopt the Resolution which is intended for submission to Her Majesty for action thereon by the United Kingdom Parliament. The *British North America Act* does not, either in terms or by implication, control this authority or require that it be subordinated to provincial assent. Nor does the *Statute of Westminster* interpose any requirement of such assent. If anything, it leaves the position as it was before its enactment. Developments subsequent thereto do not affect the legal position.

In summary, the answers to questions 1 and 3 common to the Manitoba and Newfoundland References, should be as follows:

Question 1: Yes
Question 3: As a matter of law, no.

The answer to question 4 in the Newfoundland Reference should be as expressed in the reasons of the Newfoundland Court of Appeal, subject to the correction made in the reasons herein.

The answers to the questions in the Quebec reference should be as follows:

Question A (i): Yes.
(ii): Yes.

Question B (i): As a matter of law, yes.
(ii): As a matter of law, yes.

There will be, of course, no order as to costs.

2 LEGALITY: THE MINORITY DECISION

BY JUDGES MARTLAND AND RITCHIE

IN THE MATTER of an Act for expediting the decision of constitutional and other provincial questions, being R.S.M. 1970, c. C-180

AND IN THE MATTER OF a Reference pursuant thereto by the Lieutenant Governor in Council to the Court of Appeal for Manitoba for hearing and consideration, the questions concerning the amendment of the Constitution of Canada as set out in Order in Council No. 1020/80.

THE ATTORNEY GENERAL OF MANITOBA
(Appellant)

—and—

THE ATTORNEY GENERAL OF QUEBEC
THE ATTORNEY GENERAL OF NOVA SCOTIA
THE ATTORNEY GENERAL OF BRITISH COLUMBIA
THE ATTORNEY GENERAL OF PRINCE EDWARD ISLAND
THE ATTORNEY GENERAL OF SASKATCHEWAN
THE ATTORNEY GENERAL OF ALBERTA
THE ATTORNEY GENERAL OF NEWFOUNDLAND
FOUR NATIONS CONFEDERACY INC.
(Intervenors)

—v—

THE ATTORNEY GENERAL OF CANADA
(Respondent)

46

—and—

THE ATTORNEY GENERAL OF ONTARIO
THE ATTORNEY GENERAL OF NEW BRUNSWICK
(Intervenors)

AND IN THE MATTER OF Section 6 of The Judicature Act, R.S.N. 1970, C. 187, as amended,

AND IN THE MATTER OF a Reference by the Lieutenant Governor in Council concerning the effect and validity of the amendments to the Constitution of Canada sought in the "Proposed Resolution for a Joint Address to Her Majesty The Queen respecting the Constitution of Canada"

THE ATTORNEY GENERAL OF CANADA
(Appellant)

—and—

THE ATTORNEY GENERAL OF ONTARIO
THE ATTORNEY GENERAL OF NEW BRUNSWICK
(Intervenors)

—v—

THE ATTORNEY GENERAL OF NEWFOUNDLAND
(Respondent)

—and—

THE ATTORNEY GENERAL OF QUEBEC
THE ATTORNEY GENERAL OF NOVA SCOTIA
THE ATTORNEY GENERAL OF MANITOBA
THE ATTORNEY GENERAL OF BRITISH COLUMBIA
THE ATTORNEY GENERAL OF PRINCE EDWARD IS-
LAND
THE ATTORNEY GENERAL OF SASKATCHEWAN
THE ATTORNEY GENERAL OF ALBERTA
FOUR NATIONS CONFEDERACY INC.
(intervenors)

47

AND IN THE MATTER OF a Reference to the Court of Appeal of Quebec relative to the Court of Appeal of Quebec relative to a draft Resolution containing a joint address to Her Majesty The Queen concerning the Constitution of Canada

THE ATTORNEY GENERAL OF QUEBEC
(Appellant/Respondent)
THE ATTORNEY GENERAL OF CANADA (Respondent/Appellant)
—and—

THE ATTORNEY GENERAL FOR MANITOBA
THE ATTORNEY GENERAL OF BRITISH COLUMBIA
THE ATTORNEY GENERAL OF PRINCE EDWARD ISLAND
THE ATTORNEY GENERAL OF ALBERTA
THE ATTORNEY GENERAL OF NOVA SCOTIA
THE ATTORNEY GENERAL OF SASKATCHEWAN
FOUR NATIONS CONFERACY INC.
(Intervenors supporting the Attorney General of Canada)

CORAM:
The Chief Justice and Martland, Ritchie, Dickson, Beetz, Estey, McIntyre, Chouinard and Lamer JJ.

MARTLAND and RITCHIE JJ.:

These are three appeals from the opinions of the Courts of Appeal of Manitoba, Newfoundland and Quebec pronounced in respect of three References to those Courts concerning the constitutional propriety and lawfulness of a proposed resolution now before the Senate and House of Commons of Canada.

The Lieutenant Governor in Council of Manitoba referred three questions to the Manitoba Court of Appeal for hearing and consideration by an Order in Council dated October 24, 1980; the questions were:

1. If the amendments to the Constitution of Canada sought in the 'Proposed Resolution for a Joint Address to

Her Majesty the Queen respecting the Constitution of Canada", or any of them, were enacted, would federal-provincial relationships or the powers, rights or privileges granted or secured by the Constitution of Canada to the provinces, their legislatures or governments be affected and if so, in what respect or respects?

2. Is it a constitutional convention that the House of Commons and Senate of Canada will not request Her Majesty the Queen to lay before the Parliament of the United Kingdom of Great Britain and Northern Ireland a measure to amend the Constitution of Canada affecting federal-provincial relationships or the powers, rights or privileges granted or secured by the Constitution of Canada to the provinces, their legislatures or governments without first obtaining the agreement of the provinces?

3. Is the agreement of the provinces of Canada constitutionally required for amendment to the Constitution of Canada where such amendment affects federal-provincial relationships or alters the powers, rights or privileges granted or secured by the Constitution of Canada to the provinces, their legislatures or governments?

The reasons for judgment were delivered by the Manitoba Court of Appeal on Februrary 3, 1981: (1981) 117 D.L.R. (3rd) 1; (1981) 2 W.W.R. 193. A majority of the Court refused to answer Question 1 supra. Freedman C.J.M. and Matas J.A. held that the question was at that time tentative and premature. Hall J.A. held that Question 1 was not appropriate for a judicial response, and in any event was speculative and premature. Huband and O'Sullivan JJ.A. both held that the question should have been answered in the affirmative:

Freedman C.J.M., Matas, O'Sullivan and Huband JJ.A. answered Question 2 supra in the negative. Hall J.A. held that Question 2 was not appropriate for a judicial response.

Question 3 supra was answered in the negative by Freedman C.J.M., Hall and Matas JJ.A. O'Sullivan and Huband JJ.A. would have answered Question 3 in the affirmative.

By Order in Council dated December 5, 1980, the Lieutenant Governor in Council of Newfoundland referred four questions to the Newfoundland Court of Appeal for hearing and consideration. The first three questions asked were the same as those in the Manitoba Reference. Question 4 was a follows:

4. If Part V of the proposed resolution referred to in question 1 is enacted and proclaimed into force could

(a) the Terms of Union, including terms 2 and 17 thereof contained in the Schedule to the British North America Act 1949 (12-13 George VI, c. 22 (U.K.), or

(b) section 3 of the British North America Act, 1871 (34-35 Victoria, c. 28 (U.K.)

be amended directly or indirectly pursuant to Part V without the consent of the Government, Legislature or a majority of the people of the Province of Newfoundland voting in a referendum held pursuant to Part V?

The judgment of the unanimous Court was delivered on March 31, 1981: (1981) 82 A.P.R. 503; (1981) 29 Nfld. & P.E.I.R. 503. In a joint opinion, Mifflin C.J.N., Morgan and Gushue JJ.A. answered Questions 1, 2 and 3 in the affirmative. Question 4 was answered in the following terms.

(1) By s. 3 of the *British North America Act, 1871* , Term 2 of the Terms of Union cannot now be changed without the consent of the Newfoundland Legislature.

(2) By s. 43 of the *Constitution Act* , as it now stands, none of the Terms of Union can be changed without the consent of the Newfoundland Legislative Assembly.

(3) Both of these sections can be changed by the amending formulae prescribed in s. 41 and the Term of Union could then be changed without the consent of the Newfoundland Legislature.

(4) If the amending formula under s. 42 is utilized, both of these sections can be changed by a referendum held pursuant to the provisions of s. 42. In this event, the Terms of Union could then be changed without the consent of the Newfoundland Legislature, but not without the consent of the majority of the Newfoundland people voting in a referendum.

By Order in Council dated December 17, 1980, the Government of Quebec submitted to the Quebec Court of Appeal two questions, each containing two sub-questions. The following is the English translation of the questions submitted:

A. If the Canada Act and the Constitution Act 1981 should come into force and if they should be valid in all respects in Canada would they affect:

(i) the legislative competence of the provincial legislatures in virtue of the Canadian Constitution?

(ii) the status or role of the provincial legislatures or governments within the Canadian Federation?

B. Does the Canadian Constitution empower, whether by statute, convention or otherwise, the Senate and the House of Commons of Canada to cause the Canadian Constitution to be amended without the consent of the provinces and in spite of the objection of several of them, in such a manner as to affect:

(i) the legislative competence of the provincial legislatures in virtue of the Canadian Constitution?

(ii) the status or role of the provincial legislatures or governments within the Canadian Federation?

The judgment of the Quebec Court of Appeal was delivered on April 15, 1981. Crete C.J.Q., Owen, Turgeon and Belanger JJ.A. answered both questions in the affirmative. Bisson J.A., dissenting, would have answered Question A in the affirmative and Question B in the negative.

Each of these judgments was appealed to this Court as of right. Argument was heard in this Court from the attorneys general of all ten provinces, the Attorney General of Canada, and the Four Nations Confederacy Inc. Argument was heard on each appeal, but the appeals were heard consecutively.

The *Canada Act* and the *Constitution Act, 1981*, referred to in the Quebec Reference, are the subjects of a resolution now before the Senate and House of Commons of Canada. That Resolution states:

THAT, WHEREAS in the past certain amendments to the Constitution of Canada have been made by the Parliament of the United Kingdom at the request and with the consent of Canada;

AND WHEREAS it is in accord with the status of Canada as an independent state that Canadians are able to amend their Constitution in Canada in all respects;

AND WHEREAS it is also desirable to provide in the Constitution of Canada for the recognition of certain fundamental rights and freedoms and to make other amendments to that Constitution;

A respectful address be presented to Her Majesty the Queen in the following words:

To the Queen's Most Excellent Majesty:
Most Gracious Sovereign:

We, Your Majesty's loyal subjects, the House of Commons of Canada in Parliament assembled, respectfully approach Your Majesty, requesting that you may graciously be pleased to cause to be laid before the Parliament of the United Kingdom a measure containing the recitals and clauses hereinafter set forth:

The recitals and clauses referred to in the resolution set forth the *Canada Act* and the *Constitution Act, 1981*. The *Canada Act* recites the request and consent of the Senate and House of Commons to the measure, enacts the *Constitution Act, 1981*, and declares that no Act of the Parliament of the United Kingdom passed after the *Constitution Act, 1981*, shall form part of the laws of Canada.

The *Constitution Act, 1981*, if validly enacted, would effect two major changes to the existing constitution of Canada. Part I of the Act contains a Charter of Rights and Freedoms which would bind both the Provincial and Federal legislatures. Parts IV and V of the Act contain elaborate provisions for all future amendments to the Canadian constitution.

It is now conceded that the answer to the first question in the Manitoba and Newfoundland References and to questions A (i) and (ii) of the Quebec reference should be in the affirmative. The second question in the Manitoba and Newfoundland References has been dealt with in a separate judgment to which we are parties. We agree with the disposition of the fourth question in the Newfoundland Reference proposed in the reasons for judgment of the other members of the Court which deal with that matter.

The third question in the Manitoba and the Newfoundland References asks whether the agreement of the provinces of Canada is "constitutionally required" for amendment to the Constitution of Canada where such amendment affects federal provincial relationships or alters the powers, rights or privileges granted or secured by the Constitution of Canada to the provinces, their legislatures or governments. If the second question is answered in the affirmative, then it is recognized that a constitutional convention exists that the House of Commons and the Senate will not request an amendment of the B.N.A. Act of the kind contemplated in Question 2 without first obtaining the agreement of the provinces. If that is so, then the agreement of the provinces is constitutionally required for such an amendment and the answer to Question 3 should be in the affirmative and, in our opinion, that answer should be given.

However, there is a further issue which requires consideration in that in the Courts below and in the arguments submitted by counsel before this Court, the answer to Question 3 was debated as through the words "constitutionally required" were to be considered as meaning "legally required."

In the Quebec Reference the question is phrased differently in Question B. What is asked is whether the Senate and the House of Commons are empowered by the Canadian Constitution, whether by statute, convention or otherwise, to cause the Canadian Constitution to be amended without the consent of the provinces, and in spite of the objection of several of them, in such a manner as to affect the legislative competence of Provincial Legislatures, or the status or role of provincial legislatures or governments within the Canadian Federation.

We were not referred to any statute which confers such a power. The answer to Question 2, if answered in the affirmative, denies that such a power exists by convention. The remaining issue is whether such a power has been conferred on the two Houses otherwise than by statute or convention.

We think Question B of the Quebec Reference more clearly raises the legal issue than does Question 3 in the other two References and we shall deal with that issue in these reasons.

At the outset, we would point out that we are not concerned with the matter of legality or illegality in the sense of determining whether or not the passage of the resolution under consideration involves a breach of the law. The issue is as to the existence of a power to do that which is proposed to be done. The question is whether it is *intra vires* of the Senate and the House of Commons to cause the proposed amendments to the B.N.A. Act to be made by the Imperial Parliament by means of the resolution now before the Court, in the absence of provincial agreement.

This issue is unique because in the 114 years since Confederation the Senate and House of Commons of Canada have never sought, without the consent of the Provinces, to obtain such an amendment nor, apparently, has that possibility ever been contemplated.

The *British North America Act, 1867* (herein the

B.N.A. Act) commences with the following significant recitals:

WHEREAS the Provinces of Canada, Nova Scotia and New Brunswick have expressed their Desire to be federally united into One Dominion under the Crown of the United Kingdom of Great Britain and Ireland, with a Constitution similar in Principle to that of the United Kingdom:

And whereas such a Union should conduce to the Welfare of the Provinces and promote the Interests of the British Empire:

And whereas on the Establishment of the Union by Authority of Parliament it is expedient, not only that the Constitution of the Legislative Authority in the Dominion be provided for, but also that the Nature of the Executive Government therein be declared:

And whereas it is expedient that Provision be made for the eventual Admission into the Union of other Parts of British North America:

The first recital makes it clear that this statute was passed at the behest of the named provinces and that what was sought was a federal union. The second recital states that such union would "conduce to the Welfare of the Provinces."

Parts I-V of the B.N.A. Act provide for the establishment of the Union by Proclamation, and for the vesting of executive and legislative authority in Her Majesty the Queen and Her representatives, and in the Parliament of Canada and the Legislatures of the Provinces. Part VI deals with the distribution of legislative powers. The opening words of s. 91 and s. 92 bear reproduction; they provide:

91. It shall be lawful for the Queen, by and with the Advice and Consent of the Senate and House of Commons, to make Laws for the Peace, Order and good Government of Canada, in relation to all Matters not coming within the Classes of Subjects by this Act assigned exclusively to the Legislatures of the Provinces; and for greater Certainty, but not so as to restrict the Generality of the foregoing Terms of this Section, it is hereby declared that (notwithstanding anything in this Act) the exclusive Legislative Authority of the Parliament of Canada extends to all Matters coming within the Classes of Subjects next herein-after enumerated; that is to say, —

92. In each Province the Legislature may exclusively make Laws in relation to Matters coming within the Classes of Subjects next herein-after enumerated; that is to say, ——

Section 93 gave exclusive power to the provinces to make laws in relation to education, subject to certain protective provisions in respect of denominational and separate schools.

Section 95 gave concurrent legislative power to the Provincial Legislatures and to the Parliament of Canada with respect to agriculture and immigration, but provincial legislation was to be effective only so long as it was not repugnant to an Act of the Canadian Parliament.

Part VII of the B.N.A. Act dealt with Judicature.

Part VIII dealt with revenues, debts and taxation. Section 109 provided that all lands, mines, minerals and royalties belonging to the several provinces of Canada, Nova Scotia and New Brunswick should belong to the several provinces of Ontario, Quebec, Nova Scotia and New Brunswick in which the same were situate.

Part IX is entitled "Miscellaneous Provisions." Section 129 continued all laws in effect in Canada, Nova Scotia and New Brunswick in effect at the Union, subject, except as to Acts of the Parliament of Great Britain, to repeal, abolition or alteration by the Parliament of Canada or a Provincial Legislature according to their authority under the B.N.A. Act.

Part X dealt with the Intercolonial Railway.

Part XI is concerned with the admission of other colonies. Section 146 provided:

146. It shall be lawful for the Queen, by and with the Advice of Her Majesty's Most Honourable Privy Council, on Addresses from the Houses of the Parliament of Canada, and from the Houses of the respective Legislatures of the Colonies or Provinces of Newfoundland, Prince Edward Island, and British Columbia, to admit those Colonies or Provinces, or any of them, into the Union, and on Address from the Houses of the Parliament of Canada to admit Ruupert's Land and the North-western Territory, or either of them, into the Union, on such Terms and Conditions in each Case as are in the Addresses expressed and as the Queen thinks fit to approve, subject to the Provisions of this Act; and the Provisions of any Order in Council in that Behalf shall have effect as if they had been enacted by the Parliament of the United Kingdom of Great Britain and Ireland.

This Act became the Constitution of Canada. It created a federal union of provinces and it carefully defined the respective spheres of the Canadian Parliament and the Provincial Legislatures in matters of legislative jurisdiction and property rights.

The status of the provinces under the Constitution was

determined by the Privy Council in two important cases which arose not long after the enactment of the B.N.A. Act.

It was contended in *Hodge v. The Queen*, (1883-84) 9 A.C. 117 that a Provincial Legislature could not delegate its legislative powers to License Commissioners, for it was itself merely a delegate of the Imperial Parliament. The Judicial Committee of the Privy Council rejected this argument in the following terms, at p. 32:

It appears to their Lordships, however, that the objection thus raised by the appellants is founded on an entire misconception of the true character and position of the provincial legislatures. They are in no sense delegates of or acting under any mandate from the Imperial Parliament. When the British North America Act enacted that there should be a legislature for Ontario, and that its legislative assembly should have exclusive authority to make laws for the Province and for provincial purposes in relation to the matters enumerated in sect. 92, it conferred powers not in any sense to be exercised by delegation from or as agents of the Imperial Parliament, but authority as plenary and as ample within the limits prescribed by sect. 92 as the Imperial Parliament in the plentitude of its power possessed and could bestow. Within these limits of subjects and area the local legislature is supreme, and has the same authority as the Imperial Parliament, or the Parliament of the Dominion, would have had under like circumstances to confide to a municipal institution or body of its own creation authority to make by-laws or resolutions as to subjects specified in the enactment, and with the object of carrying the enactment into operation and effect.

In *Liquidators of the Maritime Bank v. Receiver-General of New Brunswick*, (1892) A.C. 437 it was argued that the Province enjoyed no part of the Crown prerogative, and accordingly the Province of New Brunswick could not claim priority in respect of the Bank's assets for a debt owed to the Province. The argument also involved the proposition that the federal government did not share this constitutional incompetence. At p 438, counsel contended:

The prerogative rights of the Crown cannot be invoked and exercised by the provincial government, as distinguished from the Dominion Government. There is no section in the British North America Act of 1867 which gives this Crown right to the province. Accordingly, if the province possesses that right it must be on the general principle that the Lieutenant-Governor is entitled to exercise the prerogative of the Crown. But the effect of the Act of 1867 is that the Dominion Government represents the four provinces existing at the time of the Union and other provinces which were thereafter to be constituted; and, consequently, the direct connection between the Crown and the provinces has ceased. The Governor-General of Canada is the real representative of the Crown as the Dominion is at present constituted; and the Lieutenant-Governor of each province is not. Certain portions of prerogative are given to the Lieutenant-Governors, and that is inconsistent with their representing the Crown entirely. Otherwise, if the Dominion and the provinces both possess full prerogative rights you might have the Crown as representing the one contending with the Crown as representing the other.

Lord Watson spoke for the Judicial Committee and, at p 441, had this to say:

> ... They maintained that the effect of the statute has been to sever all connections between the Crown and the provinces; to make the government of the Dominion the only government of Her Majesty in North America; and to reduce the provinces to the rank of independent municipal institutions. For these propositions, which contain the sum and substance of the arguments addressed to them in support of this appeal, their Lordships have been unable to find either principle or authority.
>
> Their Lordships do not think it necessary to examine, in minute detail, the provisions of the Act of 1867, which nowhere profess to curtail in any respect the rights and privileges of the Crown, or to disturb the relations then subsisting between the Sovereign and the provinces. The object of the Act was neither to weld the provinces into one, nor to subordinate provincial governments to a central authority, but to create a federal government in which they should all be represented, entrusted with the exclusive administration of affairs in which they had a common interest, each province retaining its independence and autonomy. That object was accomplished by distributing, between the Dominion and the provinces, all powers executive and legislative, and all public property and revenues which had previously belonged to the provinces; so that the Dominion Government should be vested with such of these powers, property, and revenues as were necessary for the due performance of its constitutional functions, and that the remainder should be retained by the provinces for the purposes of provincial government. But, in so far as regards those matters which, by sect. 92, are specially reserved for provincial legislation, the legislation of each province continues to be free from the control of the Dominion, and as supreme as it was before the passing of the Act.

After quoting from the *Hodge* case included in the passage cited above, he continued:

> It is clear, therefore, that the provincial legislature of New Brunswick does not occupy the subordinate position which was ascribed to it in the argument of the appellants. It derives no authority from the Government of Canada, and its status is in no way analogous to that of a municipal institution, which is an authority constituted for purposes of local administration. It possesses powers, not of administration merely, but of legislation, in the strictest sense of that word; and, within the limits assigned by sect. 92 of the Act of 1867, these powers are exclusive and supreme. It would require very express language, such as is not to be found in the Act of 1867, to warrant the inference that the Imperial Legislature meant to vest in the provinces of Canada the right of exercising supreme legislative powers in which the British Sovereign was to have no share.

It was later established that the federal distribution of powers embraces not only legislative but also executive powers: *Bonanza Creek Gold Mining Co. v. The King,* (1916) 1 A.C. 566 at 580, per Lord Haldane. At p. 581 he said, referring to the *Maritime Bank (supra)* case:

> ...It was there laid down that "the act of the Governor-General and his Council in making the appointments is, within the meaning of the statute, the act of the Crown; and a Lieutenant-Governor, when appointed, is as much the representative of Her Majesty for all purposes of provincial government as the Governor-General himself is for all purposes of Dominion government."

The assignment of powers by the Act to the Parliament of Canada and to the Provincial Legislatures covered the whole area of self government. This was recognized by the Privy Council in *Attorney General for Ontario v. Attorney General for Canada,* (1912) A.C. 571 at 581:

> In 1867 the desire of Canada for a definite Constitution embracing the entire Dominion was embodied in the British North America Act. Now, there can be no doubt that under this organic instrument the powers distributed between the Dominion on the one hand and the provinces on the other hand cover the whole area of self-government within the whole area of Canada. It would be subversive of the entire scheme and policy of the Act to assume that any point of internal self-government was withheld from Canada.

In *Murphy v. Canadian Pacific Railway Company,* (1958) S.C.R. 626 Rand J. stated:

> . . .It has become a truism that the totality of effective legislative power is conferred by the Act of 1867, subject always to the express or necessarily implied limitation of the Act itself.

The foregoing review shows that the enactment of the B.N.A. Act created a federal constitution of Canada which confided the whole area on self government within Canada to the Parliament of Canada and the Provincial Legislatures each being supreme within its own defined sphere and area. It can fairly be said, therefore, that the dominant principle of Canadian constitutional law is federalism. The implications of that principle are clear. Each level of government should not be permitted to encroach on the other, either directly or indirectly. The political compromise achieved as a result of the Quebec and London Conferences preceding the passage of the B.N.A. Act would be dissolved unless there were substantive and effective limits on unconstitutional action.

The B.N.A. Act did not make any specific provision as to the means of determining the constitutionality of any federal or provincial legislation. That task has been assumed and performed by the courts, with supreme authority initially resting with the Judicial Committee of the Privy Council and, since, 1949, with this Court.

In performing this function, the courts, in addition to dealing with cases involving alleged excesses of legislative jurisdiction, have had occasion to develop legal principles based on the necessity of preserving the integrity of the federal structure. We will be dealing with these later in this judgment. We will, however, at this point cite one instance of the performance of this task in the following case by the Privy Council.

In *Attorney General for Canada v. Attorney General for Ontario,* (1937) A.C. 326 (the *Labour Conventions* case) the issue was as to the constitutional validity of three federal statutes enacted in 1935 dealing with labour matters, such as weekly rest in industrial undertakings, hours of work and minimum wages. In substance, they gave effect to draft conventions adopted by the International Labour Organization of the League of Nations in accordance with the Labour Pact of the Treaty of Versailles, 1919, ratified by Canada. For the Attorney General for Canada it was argued that the legislation was valid because it was for the purpose of performing Canadian treaty obligations. For the Province it was contended that the statutes related to property and civil rights in the Province.

The argument made on behalf of the Attorney General for Canada, as reported at p. 330, was very similar to the submissions made for the Attorney General of Canada in this case:

...By the transference of the treaty-making power to the Dominion executive, and correlative power to legislate to carry out the obligations, nothing is taken from the Provinces.
(Lord Atkin. The Dominion has not got unlimited powers of legislation.)

The residuary clause of s. 91 of the British North America Act is capable of the construction, which is not inconsistent with decided cases, that where Canada has properly incurred an international obligation with respect to any matter whatsoever, that within whatever classes in ss. 91 and 92 it may be described as coming under other circumstances, once the matter has assumed the aspect of an international bargain it is no longer to be treated as belonging to any one of the enumerated classes.
(Lord Atkin. That is a very far-reaching doctrine: it means that Canada could make an agreement with any State which would seriously affect Provincial rights.)

It is a power which cannot be exercised by Canada alone; some other country must be found which is willing to enter into a bargain. This matter must not be looked at as though Canada is going to look about the world to find some one with whom to make an agreement for the purpose of robbing the Provinces of their constitutional rights. But, logically, it must be admitted that whatever Canada and such other country agree to can be effected by Canada.

This argument was rejected not only on the basis that

there was no support for it in the constitution itself, but also because of its incompatibility with the federal structure of government in Canada. At pp. 351-53, Lord Atkin said:

> For the purposes of ss. 91 and 92, i.e., the distribution of legislative powers between the Dominion and the Provinces, there is no such thing as treaty legislation as such. The distribution is based on classes of subjects; and as a treaty deals with a particular class of subjects so will the legislative power of performing it be ascertained. No one can doubt that this distribution is one of the most essential conditions, probably the most essential condition, in the interprovincial compact to which the British North America Act gives effect. If the position of Lower Canada, now Quebec, alone were considered, the existence of her separate jurisprudence as to both property and civil rights might be said to depend upon loyal adherence to her constitutional right to the exclusive competence of her own Legislature in these matters. Nor is it of less importance for the other Provinces, though their law may be based on English jurisprudence, to preserve their own right to legislate for themselves in respect of local conditions which may vary by as great a distance as separates the Atlantic from the Pacific. It would be remarkable that while the Dominion could not initiate legislation, however desirable, which affected civil rights in the Provinces, yet its Government not responsible to the Provinces nor controlled by Provincial Parliaments need only agree with a foreign country to enact such legislation, and its Parliament would be forthwith clothed with authority to affect Provincial rights to the full extent of such agreement. Such a result would appear to undermine the constitutional safeguards of Provincial constitutional autonomy.
>
> It follows from what has been said that no further legislative competence is obtained by the Dominion from its accession to international status, and the consequent increase in the scope of its executive functions. It is true, as pointed out in the judgment of the Chief Justice, that as the executive is now clothed with the powers of making treaties so the Parliament of Canada, to which the executive is responsible, has imposed upon it responsibilities in connection with such treaties, for if it were to disapprove of them they would either not be made or the Ministers would meet their constitutional fate. But this is true of all executive functions in their relation to Parliament. There is no existing constitutional ground for stretching the competence of the Dominion Parliament so that it becomes enlarged to keep pace with enlarged functions of the Dominion executive. If the new functions affect the classes of subjects enumerated in s. 92 legislation to support the new functions is in the competence of the Provincial Legislatures only. If they do not, the competence of the Dominion Legislature is declared by s. 91 and existed ab origine. In other words, the Dominion cannot, merely by making promises to foreign countries, clothe itself with legislative authority inconsistent with the constitution which gave it birth.

There are several features of the *Labour Conventions* case which require emphasis. The federal government was in that case asserting the right to enact legislation which was within provincial authority in order to carry out the treaty obligations which it had assumed. No question was raised as to the validity of the federal governments authority to negotiate and ratify international treaties. What was held unconstitutional by the Privy Council was the use of that lawful procedure to legislate indirectly beyond the powers invested in the federal parliament by s. 91 of the B.N.A. Act.

In these appeals this Court is equally concerned with the exercise of a valid power, namely, the power of the federal Houses of Parliament to pass resolutions requesting amendments to the B.N.A. Act. That power has historic foundation, but we note that it has never before been exercised for the purpose of curtailing provincial legislative authority without provincial consent. In the context of the Labour Conventions case, the issue in these appeals is whether the established incompetence of the federal government to encroach on provincial powers can be avoided through the use of the resolution procedure to effect a constitutional amendment passed at the behest of the federal government by the Parliament of the United Kingdom.

The only provisions of the B.N.A. Act dealing with amendments to the constitution are as follows. Head 1 of s. 92 empowered a Provincial Legislature to make laws in relation to:

1. The Amendment from Time to Time, notwithstanding anything in this Act, of the Constitution of the Province, except as regards the Office of Lieutenant Governor.

Section 146, already cited, made provision for the admission of other colonies and territories into the Union.

By an amendment made in 1949 to s. 91 of the B.N.A. Act, a limited power of amendment was given to the Federal Parliament. Head 1 of s. 91 enabled it to legislate in relation to:

1. The amendment from time to time of the Constitution of Canada, except as regards matters coming within the classes of subjects by this Act assigned exclusively to the Legislatures of the provinces, or as regards rights or privileges by this or any other Constitutional Act granted or secured to the Legislature or the Government of a province, or to any class of persons with respect to schools or as regards the use of the English or the French language or as regards the requirements that there shall be a session of the Parliament of Canada at least once each year, and that no House of Commons shall continue for more than five years from the day of the return of the Writs for choosing the House: provided, however, that a House of Commons may in time of real or apprehended war, invasion or insurrection be continued by the Parliament of Canada if such continuation is not opposed by the votes of more than one-third of the members of such House.

This provision specifically excepted from its operation, *inter alia*, matters coming within the classes of subjects assigned exclusively to the Provinces. The scope of s. 91.1 was considered by this Court in *Re: Authority of Parliament in Relation to the Upper House*, (1980) 1 S.C.R. 54 (herein the Senate Reference). In that case, this Court unanimously held that the federal government could not, acting under s. 91.1, abolish the Senate. The term "Constitution of Canada" found in s. 91.1 was held in its context to refer only to the federal juristic unit. It is significant that when, as recently as 1949, the Houses of Parliament sought and obtained a provision permitting the Federal Parliament sought and obtained a provision permitting the Federal Parliament to amend the constitution by legislation, specific provision was made to ensure that this power was not capable of implying any right to interfere with those powers assigned to the Provinces by the B.N.A. Act.

Because the Canadian Constitution was created by the B.N.A. Act in the form of an Imperial statute, it followed that in the absence of a provision for amendment within it, its amendment could only be effected by the enactment of an Imperial statute. Over the years many amendments have occurred in this way. The practice has developed, since 1895, to have the formal approach to the Imperial Parliament made by means of a joint address of both Houses of Parliament. This form of procedure had been followed earlier in respect of amendments to the *Act of Union, 1840.*
It is also the procedure spelled out in s. 146 of the B.N.A. Act as the means of approach to the Queen, acting on the advice of her Privy Council for the admission of existing colonies, or territories, into the Union.

The record of constitutional amendments passed since 1867 by the Imperial Parliament is contained in the Favreau White Paper of 1965, issued by the federal government, and approved by the provincial governments. It was cited by this court in the Senate Reference. Many of these amendments concerned mere formalities, such as the postponement of redistribution of seats in the House of Commons in 1916 and 1943 to await the cessation of hostilities. Those amendments which were important in relation to the proper procedure for amendment were discussed in that Paper, and we think they bear repetition in full:

(1) *The British North America Act of 1871* —

(Established of new provinces
and administration of territories)

Because this was the first attempt by Canada to have the Constitution amended, there were no precedents for the government of the day to follow. It requested the amendment from the British Parliament without reference to the Parliament of Canada, and the latter took strong exception. The opposition in Parliament condemned the government for its failure to secure prior approval of Canada's legislative authority. The government agreed that such matters should be referred to Parliament, and the House of Commons unanimously adopted a resolution stating that ". . . no changes in the provisions of the British North America Act (would) be sought by the Executive Government without the previous assent of the Parliament of this Dominion." A few days later, the government brought down a joint Address, which was concurred in by both Houses of Parliament, and which formed the basis upon which the amendment was finally passed by the British Parliament.

(2) *The Parliament of Canada Act, 1875* —

(Privileges, immunities and powers
of the House of Parliament)

Notwithstanding the principle it has pressed for, and had had unanimously adopted by Parliament four years earlier when it was in opposition, the Canadian government of the day requested this amendment without "previous assent" or formal Address by Parliament.

Objections again were raised in the House of Commons and a resolution similar to that of 1871 was introduced. After debate, the government conceded the propriety of the principle it had originally espoused: of referring proposed constitutional amendments to Parliament. The new resolution was withdrawn when the government agreed that a joint Address by both Houses of Parliament was the only appropriate way of securing amendments to the Constitution.

(3) *The British North America Act of 1886* —

(Respresentation of territories in Parliament)

The Canadian government submitted its request for this amendment to Westminster on the basis of a formal Address by both Houses of Parliament. With one exception, this principle has been followed by every Canadian government since that time. The exception was the enactment in 1895 by the United Kingdom Parliament of the Canadian Speaker (Appointment of Deputy) Act, which was allowed without protest by the Canadian Parliament because of particular circumstances.

(4) *The British North America Act of 1907* —

(Subsidies to provinces)

This was the first occasion on which the federal government consulted with the provinces before seeking a constitutional amendment. In this case, all nine of the provinces in existence were directly concerned with the amendment. All were consulted and eight of the nine provincial governments agreed to the federal proposal. One province opposed the proposal, both in Canada and in Great Britain. The British government made minor changes in the text of the draft bill, and the amendment was enacted.

63

(5) *The British North America Act of 1915* —

(Redefinition of divisions of the Senate)

This amendment was passed without consultation with the provinces and without provincial government representations concerning its enactment. This amendment is important to Canadian constitutional development in that it was put forward in the form of a Canadian draft bill, embodied in the Address to the Crown and enacted without modification by the British Parliament.

(6) *The British North America Act of 1930* —

(Jurisdiction of Western provinces
over their natural resources)

This was the first application for a constitutional amendment relating to a provincial field that did not directly concern all provinces. It was obtained by the federal government after consultation with only those provinces directly affected except in one province where a resolution was adopted by the legislature after the Premier had already expressed the consent of his government to the amendment.

(7) *The British North America Act of 1940* —

(Unemployment Insurance)

This was the first amendment to change the distribution of legislative powers between Parliament and the provinces, as provided in the 1867 Constitution. It transferred the authority to legislate on unemployment insurance from provincial to federal jurisdiction. Before seeking this amendment, the federal government obtained the consent of all provincial governments, In this, as in previous cases of provincial concurrence, there was no reference of the question by any government to its legislature.

(8) *The British North America Act of 1943* —

(Postponement of redistribution
of seats in the House of Commons)

The federal government did not consult the provinces prior to seeking this amendment, and notwithstanding the protest of one provincial government, the Parliament of the United Kingdom granted it. The position of the federal government was that this amendment concerned only the Government of Canada, since it did not affect provincial governments or legislatures.

(9) *The British North America Act of 1946* —

(Readjustment of representation
in the House of Commons)

The federal government sought this amendment on the same basis as that of 1943 — that is, without provincial consultations — and for the same reasons.

(10) *The British North America Act of 1949* —

(Entry of Newfoundland into Confederation)

A resolution was moved in the House of Commons urging that this amendment not be proceeded with until after consultation with the provincial governments. What the resolution meant by "consultation" was not clear. However, the amendment was enacted without such consultation and without any of the provincial governments formally objecting to its enactment, though one or two provincial governments stated publicly that consultation should have taken place.

(11) *The British North America Act of 1949(2)* —

(Authority of Parliament to amend certain
aspects of the Constitution of Canada)

This amendment was obtained without consultation or formal consent of provincial governments, the federal government maintaining the position taken in connection with the 1943 and 1946 amendments. At a federal-provincial constitutional conference the following year, however, the federal government indicated that, in the event of agreement on an overall procedure for amending the Constitution of Canada, it would be prepared to reconsider the broad provisions of this amendment.

(12) *The British North America Act of 1951* —

(Old Age Pensions)

This amendment was enacted after the federal government secured the agreement of all provinces. In the case of the provinces of Quebec, Saskatchewan and Manitoba, the matter was referred to the legislatures, which authorized the governments of those provinces to agree to the amendment. Other provincial governments gave concurrence on their own authority.

(13) *The British North America Act of 1960* —

(Tenure of office of certain Judges)

The federal government sought this amendment only after obtaining the agreement of all provinces, since the amendment provided for the compulsory retirement at age 75 of judges of provincial courts. In this instance again Quebec placed the matter before its legislature before agreeing.

(14) *The British North America Act of 1964* —

(Supplementary benefits to Old Age Pensions)

This amendment was enacted after agreement of all provincial governments, with, in the case of Quebec, the concurrence of the Legislative Assembly. It involved a modification of section 94A created by the 1951 amendment on which prior agreement of all provinces had been obtained.

65

The Favreau White Paper goes on to say:

There have been five instances — in 1907, 1940, 1951, 1960 and 1964 — of
federal consultation with all provinces on matters of direct concern to all of
them. There has been only one instance up to the present time in which an
amendment was sought after consultation with only those provinces directly affected by it. This was the amendment of 1930, which transferred to the
Western provinces natural resources that had been under the control of the
federal government since their admission to Confederation. There have
been ten instances (in 1871, 1875, 1886, 1895, 1915, 1916, 1943, 1946, 1949 and
1949 (2)) of amendments to the Constitution without prior consultation with
the provinces on matters that the federal government considered were of
exclusive federal concern. In the last four of these, one or two provinces
protested that federal-provincial consultations should have taken place pri-
or to action by Parliament.

In no instance has an amendment to the B.N.A. Act
been enacted which directly affected federal-provincial relationships in the sense of changing provincial legislative powers, in the absence of federal consultation with and the consent of all the provinces. Notably, this procedure continued
to be followed in the four instances which occurred after the
enactment of the *Statute of Westminster* (herein the Statute of Westminster).

This history of amendments reveals the operation of
constitutional constraints. While the choice of the resolution
procedure is itself a matter of internal parliamentary responsibility, the making of the addresses to the Sovereign
falls into two areas. Resolutions concerning the federal
juristic unit and federal powers were made without reference to any but the members of the federal Houses. Resolutions abridging provincial authority have never been passed
without the concurrence of the Provinces. In other words,
the normal constitutional principles recognizing the inviola-
bility of separate and exclusive legislative powers were carried into and considered an integral part of the operation of
the resolution procedure.

The history of constitutional amendments also parallels
the development of Canadian sovereignty. The B.N.A. Act
did not have among its purposes the severance of Canada
from the British Commonwealth. However, the vital role of
Canadian consent as an expression of Canadian sovereignty
is revealed in the fact that no constitutional amendment has
been passed without that consent.

The Statute of Westminster was enacted following two
Imperial Conferences held in 1926 and 1930, attended by rep-

resentatives of the United Kingdom, Canada, Australia, New Zealand, South Africa, the Irish Free State and Newfoundland. At the earlier conference, the established constitutional position was stated in a form which has come to be called the "Balfour Declaration":

They are autonomous communities within the British Empire, equal in status, in no way subordinate one to another in any aspect of their domestic or external affairs, though united by a common allegiance to the Crown, and freely associated as members of the British Commonwealth.

The Statute of Westminster was enacted to give effect in the law of the United Kingdom to the established fact of sovereign status of the communities within the British Empire.

The following provisions of the Statute were referred to in argument before us:

2. (1) The Colonial Laws Validity Act, 1865, shall not apply to any law made after the commencement of this Act by the Parliament of a Dominion.

(2) No law and no provision of any law made after the commencement of this Act by the Parliament of a Dominion shall be void or inoperative on the ground that it is repugnant to the law of England, or to the provisions of any existing or future Act of Parliament of the United Kingdom, or to any order, rule, or regulation made under any such Act, and the powers of the Parliament of a Dominion shall include the power to repeal or amend any such Act, order, rule or regulation in so far as the same is part of the law of the Dominion.

3. It is hereby declared and enacted that the Parliament of a Dominion has full power to make laws having extra-territorial operation.

4. No Act of Parliament of the United Kingdom passed after the commencement of this Act shall extend or be deemed to extend, to a Dominion as part of the law of that Dominion, unless it is expressly declared in that Act that that Dominion has requested, and consented to, the enactment thereof.

. . .

7. (1) Nothing in this Act shall be deemed to apply to the repeal, amendment or alteration of the British North America Acts, 1867 to 1930, or any order, rule or regulation made thereunder.

(2) The provisions of section two of this Act shall extend to laws made by any of the Provinces of Canada and to the powers of the legislatures of such Provinces.

(3) The powers conferred by this Act upon the Parliament of Canada or upon the legislatures of the Provinces shall be restricted to the enactment of laws in relation to matters within the competence of the Parliament of Canada or of any of the legislatures of the Provinces respectively.

We do not regard s.4 as having any real impact on the matter in issue in these appeals. The section uses the word "extend" and we therefore regard the section as meaning that a United Kingdom statute would not, in the absence of the declaration referred to in the section, be a part of the law of any Dominion. It is, however, of interest that each of the amendments made after the Statute of Westminster took effect contains a declaration that the enactment had been requested and consented to by Canada.

Of the Dominions to which the Statute of Westminster applied, all were unitary states except Canada and Australia, and the Australian constitution already contained provision for its amendment.

In relation to Canada, the possible impact of s. 2 was a cause of concern to the Provinces because it could be construed as enabling the Federal Parliament to repeal or amend the B.N.A. Act. The origin of s. 7 was the result of that concern. The Favreau White Paper at pp. 18-19 deals with the history of this section:

On June 30th, 1931, the Right Honourable R. B. Bennett, Prime Minister of Canada, introduced in the House of Commons a resolution for an Address to His Majesty requesting the enactment of the Statute of Westminster. The preamble to the resolution said:

"And whereas consideration has been given by the proper authorities in Canada as to whether and to what extent the principles embodied in the proposed act of the parliament of the United Kingdom should be applied to provincial legislation; and, at a dominion-provincial conference, held at Ottawa on the seventh and eighth days of April, in the year of Our Lord one thousand nine hundred and thirty-one, a clause was approved by the delegates of His Majesty's government in Canada and of the governments of all of the provinces of Canada, for insertion in the proposed act for the purpose of providing that the provisions of the proposed act relating to the Colonial Laws Validity Act should extend to laws made by the provinces of Canada and to the powers of the legislatures of the provinces; and also for the purpose of providing that nothing in the proposed act should be deemed to apply to the repeal, amendment or alteration of the British North America Acts of 1867 to 1930; or any order, rule or regulation made thereunder; and also for the purpose of providing that the powers conferred by the proposed act on the parliament of Canada and upon the legislatures of the provinces should be restricted to the enactment of the parliament of Canada or any of the legislatures of the provinces respectively."

The Prime Minister explained that the Dominion-Provincial Conference referred to in the preamble had been convened in response to representations by Ontario, subsequently supported by the other provinces. He referred to the apprehension of some of the provinces that under provisions as broad as those to be inserted in the Statute of Westminster, a dominion parliament might encroach upon the jurisdiction of a provincial legislature and exercise powers beyond its competence. He pointed out that ". . .lest it be concluded by inference that the rights of the provinces as defined by the British North America Act had been by reason of this Statute curtailed, lessened, modified or repealed," a section of the Statute of special application to Canada declared, with the unanimous concurrence of the provinces, that such was not the case.

The Statute of Westminster was passed on December 11, 1931. Earlier that year, Mr. Louis St. Laurent, then President of the Canadian Bar Association, and a distinguished constitutional lawyer, referred in his presidential address, reported in 9 Canadian Bar Review, p. 525, to the resolutions of the House of Commons and the Senate requesting the enactment of the Statute. This speech was not delivered in a political context. At that time he did not hold any political office. It was some years later that he became a Member of the House of Commons and a Minister of the Crown. The following passage from that speech is relevant to the issue now before the Court:

> Now, it may be that while both the Dominion and the Provinces remained subject to the legislative jurisdiction of His Majesty's Parliament of the United Kingdom, that Parliament had, in theory, full power to vary the distribution of legislative jurisdiction between them. But after the declaration of 1926 that both the United Kingdom and the Dominions are autonomous communities equal in status, in no way subordinate one to another in any aspect of their domestic or external affairs, it would hardly seem probable that the Parliament of the United Kingdom would undertake to legislate for the territory of any one of those Dominions, unless it be expressly declared in the Act that that Dominion had requested and consented to the enactment for the proposed legislation. And if the United Kingdom and the Dominions are equal in status and in no way subordinate one to another in any aspect of their domestic or external affairs, does not the provision of section 92 of the Act of 1867, that in each province the legislature may exclusively make laws in relation to the amendment from time to time of its constitution, except as regards the office of Lieutenant-Governor, seem to indicate that the Houses of the Dominion Parliament would have no jurisdiction to request or to consent to enactmments that might extend or abridge Provincial legislative autonomy? It is true that one of the proposed sub-sections of the Statute of Westminster is to declare that nothing in that Statute shall be deemed to apply to the repeal, amendment or alteration of the British North America Acts, 1867 to 1930, or any other, rule or regulation made thereunder; but the declaration of the Imperial Conference purports to be a statement of the established constitutional position, and if it is so in fact, is anything further required to make it clear that the constitution of the provinces can be amended or affected only by the provinces themselves?
>
> Section 92 excludes federal jurisdiction over them, and the declaration of 1926 does seem to state a constitutional position that precludes interference with them by any other Parliament to which they are said to be no way subordinate.

The Statute of Westminster gave statutory recognition to the independent sovereign status of Canada as a nation. However, while Canada, as a nation, was recognized as being sovereign, the government of the nation remained federal in character and the Frederal Parliament did not acquire sole control of the exercise of that sovereignty. Section 2 of the Statute of Westminster, standing alone, could be construed as giving that control to the Federal Parliament, but the enactment of s. 7, at the instance of the Provinces, was intended to preclude that exercise of power by the Federal Parliament. Subsection 7(3) in particular gave explicit recognition to the continuation of the division of powers created by the B.N.A. Act. The powers conferred on the Parliament of Canada by the Statute of Westminster were restricted to the enactment of laws in relation to matters within the competence of the Parliament of Canada.

The effect of s. 7(1) was to preserve the Imperial Parliament as the legal instrument for enacting amendments to the B.N.A. Acts, 1867-1930. This clearly had no effect on the existing procedure which had been used to obtain the amendment of the B.N.A. Act. The resolution procedure, which, after 1895, had produced all the constitutional amendments until 1931, has been followed in respect of all the constitutional amendments passed since 1931.

The Attorney General of Canada presented a deceptively simple argument in support of the legality of the resolution at issue in these appeals. It was argued that the resolution is not a law, and therefore not a proper subject for judicial consideration and, further, that the two Houses can legally pass any resolution which they desire. The Imperial parliament has full legal authority to amend the B.N.A. Act by enacting a statute, and its power to do so cannot be questioned. If, therefore, the Imperial Parliament enacts such a statute in response to a resolution of the Senate and the House of Commons, there can be no question of illegality.

However, it was also submitted that while the Imperial Parliament has full legal authority to amend the B.N.A. Act, there exists a "firm and unbending" convention that such an amendment will only be enacted in response to a resolution of the two Houses requesting it, and, further, that it will enact any amendment to the B.N.A. Act which is so requested.

In the result, if this process is examined from the point of view of substance rather than of form, what is being asserted is the existence of a power in the Senate and the House of Commons to cause any amendment to the B.N.A. Act which they desire to be enacted, even though that amendment subtracts, without provincial consent, from the legislative powers of the Provinces granted to them by the B.N.A. Act.

In support of the proposition that resolutions are questions of internal parliamentary procedure and are not proper subjects of judical consideration, reference was made to two British authors. In his *Introduction to the Study of the Law of the Constitution* (10th ed.), Dicey states at pp. 54-55 that the resolution of neither House is law and each House has complete control over its own proceedings. May's *Parliamentary Practice* (18th ed.) at p. 195 affirms the rule that each House has exclusive jurisdiction over its own internal proceedings.

The English authorities, such as Dicey and May, respecting the power of the Houses of Parliament to pass resolutions, and as to their effect, are related to resolutions of the Houses of Parliament in a unitary state. Under the British constitution, the only limitation on the power of Parliament is that its authority must be expressed in legislation. Any 'constitutional amendment' under the British constitution can be passed by normal legislation. Accordingly, these authorities are of no help in determining the limitations, if any, on the authority of one level of government in a federal state, respecting the use of an accepted amending procedure for the purpose of abridging the powers of the other legislative level. The resolution under consideration is not a matter of internal procedure. A resolution of the Senate and the House of Commons has become recognized as the means whereby a request is made to the Imperial Parliament for legislation to effect a constitutional amendment.

The power of the Senate and the House of Commons to pass resolutions of any kind, and to use such resolutions for any purpose, was stated by the Attorney General to have been recognized in s. 18 of the B.N.A. Act and s. 4 of the Senate and House of Commons Act, R.S.C. 1970, c. S-8. Section 18 of the B.N.A. Act provides:

18. The privileges, immunities, and powers to be held, enjoyed, and exercised by the Senate and by the House of Commons, and by the Members thereof respectively, shall be such as are from time to time defined by Act of the Parliament of Canada, but so that any Act of the Parliament of Canada defining such privileges, immunities, or powers exceeding those at the passing of such Act held, enjoyed, and exercised by the Commons House of Parliament of the United Kingdom of Great Britain and Ireland, and by the Members thereof.

Section 18 in its present form was enacted by the *Parliament of Canada Act, 1875* , to replace s. 18 of the B.N.A. Act, 1867. The difference in phraseology of the two sections is not relevant to the matter in issue in these appeals.

Section 18 did not, in itself, create or recognize the existence of the privileges, immunities and powers of the Senate and the House of Commons. It provided that their privileges, immunities and powers should be such as are, from time to time, defined by Act of the Parliament of Canada, subject to the limitation that Parliament could not by statute, give to the Senate or the House of Commons any privileges, immunities or powers which exceeded those enjoyed by the House of Commons of the United Kingdom Parliament. Parliament could not grant legislative powers to its two Houses. Furthermore, because, unlike the Parliament of the United Kingdom, Parliament's power to legislate was limited in extent, it could not grant to the Senate and the House of Commons powers which it did not itself possess.

In the exercise of the power granted to it by s. 18 of the B.N.A. Act, the Parliament of Canada, in 1868, passed an Act to define the privileges, immunities and powers of the Senate and House of Commons, S.C. 1868, c. 23. Sections 1 and 2 of that Act provided as follows:

1. The Senate and the House of Commons respectively, and the Members thereof respectively, shall hold, enjoy and exercise such and the like privileges, immunities and powers as, at the time of the passing of the British North America Act, 1867, were held, enjoyed and exercised by the Commons House of Parliament of the United Kingdom of Great Britain and Ireland, and by the Members thereof, so far as the same are consistent with and not repugnant to the said Act.

2. Such privileges, immunities and powers shall be deemed to be and shall be part of the General and Public Law of Canada, and it shall not be necessary to plead the same, but the same shall in all Courts in Canada and by and before all Judges be taken notice of judicially.

The essential provisions of these two sections were repeated in subsequent legislation. They now appear in sections 4 and 5 of the *Senate and House of Commons Act* , R.S.C. 1970, c. S-8, as follows:

4. The Senate and the Houses of Commons respectively, and the members thereof respectively, hold, enjoy and exercise,

(a) such and the like privileges, immunities and powers as, at the time

72

of the passing of the British North America Act, 1867, were held, enjoyed and exercised by the Commons House of Parliament of the United Kingdom, and by the members thereof, so far as the same are consistent with and not repugnant to that Act; and

(b) such privileges, immunities and powers as are from time to time defined by Act of the Parliament of Canada, not exceeding those at the time of the passing of such Act held, enjoyed and exercised by the Commons House of Parliament of the United Kingdom and by the members thereof respectively.

5. Such privileges, immunities and powers are part of the general and public law of Canada, and it is not necessary to plead the same, but the same shall, in all courts in Canada, and by and before all judges, be taken notice of judicially.

Parliament did not confer upon the Senate and the House of Commons all of the privileges, immunities and powers held, enjoyed and exercised by the House of Commons of the United Kingdom, but only conferred them "so far as the same are consistent with and not repugnant to that Act", i.e. the B.N.A. Act, 1867. It thus recognized that some powers enjoyed by the House of Commons of the United Kingdom might not be consistent with the provisions of the B.N.A. Act.

In our opinion this very important proviso took into account the fact that, whereas the House of Commons in the United Kingdom was one of the Houses in the Parliament of a unitary state, the Canadian Senate and House of Commons were Houses in a Parliament in a federal state, whose powers were not all embracing, but were specifically limited by the Act which created it.

In order to pass the resolution now under consideration the Senate and the House of Commons must purport to exercise a power. The source of that power must be found in paragraph 4(a) of the *Senate and House of Commons Act* , since there has been no legislation enacted to date, other than paragraph 4(a) which actually defines the privileges, immunities and powers upon the two Houses of Parliament. The resolution now before us was passed for the purpose of obtaining an amendment to the B.N.A. Act, the admitted effect of which is to curtail Provincial legislative powers under s. 92 of the B.N.A. Act. In our opinion that power is not consistent with the B.N.A. Act but is repugnant to it. It is a power which is out of harmony with the very basis of the B.N.A. Act. Therefore paragraph (a) of s. 4, because of the limitations which it contains, does not confer that power. The Senate and the House of Commons are purporting to exercise a power which they do not possess.

The effect of the position taken by the Attorney General of Canada is that the two Houses of Parliament have unfettered control of a triggering mechanism by means of which they can cause the B.N.A. Act to be amended in any way they desire. It was frankly conceded in argument that there were no limits of any kind upon the type of amendment that could be made in this fashion. In our opinion, this argument in essence maintains that the Provinces have since, at the latest 1931, owed their continued existence not to their constitutional powers expressed in the B.N.A. Act, but to the Federal Parliament's sufferance. While the Federal Parliament was throughout this period incompetent to legislate in respect of matters assigned to the Provinces by s. 92, its two Houses could at any time have done so by means of a resolution to the Imperial Parliament, procuring an amendment to the B.N.A. Act.

The Attorney General of Canada, in substance, is asserting the existence of a power in the two Houses of Parliament to obtain amendments to the B.N.A. Act which could disturb and even destroy the federal system of constitutional government in Canada. We are not aware of any possible legal source for such a power. The House of Commons and the Senate are part of the Parliament of Canada. Section 17 of the B.N.A. Act states that there "shall be one Parliament for Canada, consisting of the Queen, an Upper House styled the Senate and the House of Commons". Laws under s. 91 of the B.N.A. Act are enacted by the Queen, with the advice and consent of the Senate and House of Commons. These two constituents of Parliament cannot by themselves enact legislation, nor could Parliament clothe them with powers beyond those possessed by Parliament itself.

The Attorney General of Canada contends that because subs. 7(1) of the Statute left the repeal, amendment or alteration of the *British North America Acts 1867* to *1930* in the hands of the Imperial Parliament, there is nothing to prevent the two Houses of Parliament from requesting that an amendment be made in whatever form they submit. This submission means that the two Houses of Parliament can accomplish, indirectly, through the intervention of the Imperial Parliament, that which the Parliament of Canada itself is unable to do. In our opinion, the two Houses lack legal authority, of their own motion, to obtain constitutional amendments which would strike at the very basis of the Canadian federal system, i.e. the complete division of legislative powers between the Parliament of Canada and the Provincial Legislatures. It is the duty of this Court to consider this assertion of rights with a view to the preservation of the Constitution.

This Court, since its inception, has been active in reviewing the constitutionality of both Federal and Provincial legislation. This role has generally been concerned with the interpretation of the express terms of the B.N.A. Act. However, on occasions, this Court has had to consider issues for which the B.N.A. Act offered no answer. In each case, this Court has denied the assertion of any power which would offend against the basic principles of the Constitution.

In *Amax Potash Limited et al v. The Government of Saskatchewan* , (1977) 2 S.C.R. 576 plaintiff sued for a declaration that certain sections of *The Mineral Taxation Act* , R.S.S. 1965, c. 64, and certain regulations made pursuant to that Act, were *ultra vires* and sought the recovery of moneys paid by way of tax under the regulations. The Government of Saskatchewan disputed the contention that these provisions were ultra vires, but also contended that no cause of action was disclosed because subs. 5(7) of *The Proceedings against the Crown Act* , R.S.S. 1965, c. 87, was a bar to the recovery of moneys paid to the Crown. The relevant part of subs. 5(7) provided:

> 5. (7) No proceedings lie against the Crown under this or any other section of the Act in respect to anything heretofore or hereafter done or omitted and purporting to have been done or omitted in the exercise of a power or authority under a statute or a statutory provision purporting to confer or to have conferred on the Crown such power or authority, which statute or statutory provision is or was or may be beyond the legislative jurisdiction of the Legislature.

In the course of his reasons, Dickson J., who delivered the judgement of the Court, said at p. 590:

> A state, it is said, is sovereign and it is not for the Courts to pass upon

the policy or wisdom of legislative will. As a broad statement of principle that is undoubtedly correct, but the general principle must yield to the requisites of the constitution in a federal state. By it the bounds of sovereignty are defined and supremacy circumscribed. The Courts will not question the wisdom of enactments which, by the terms of the Canadian Constitution are within the competence of the Legislatures, but it is the high duty of this Court to insure that the Legislatures do not transgress the limits of their constitutional mandate and engage in the illegal exercise of power. Both Saskatchewan and Alberta inform the Court that justice and equity are irrelevant in this case. If injustice results, it is the electorate which must administer a rebuke, and not the Courts. The two Provinces apparently find nothing inconsistent or repellent in the contention that a subject can be barred from recovery of sums paid to the Crown under protest, in response to the compulsion of the legislation later found to be *ultra vires* .

Section 5(7) of *The Proceedings against the Crown Act* , in my opinion, has much broader implications than mere Crown immunity. In the present context, it directly concerns the right to tax. It affects, therefore, the division of powers under *The British North America Act, 1867* . It also brings into question the right of a Province, or the federal Parliament for that matter, to act in violation of the Canadian Constitution. Since it is manifest that if either the federal Parliament of a provincial Legislature can tax beyond the limit of its powers, and by prior or *ex post facto* legislation give itself immunity from such illegal act, it could readily place itself in the same position as if the act had been done within proper constitutional limits. To allow moneys collected under compulsion, pursuant to an *ultra vires* statute, to be retained would be tantamount to allowing the provincial Legislature to do indirectly what it could not do directly, and by covert means to impose illegal burdens.

In *British Columbia Power Corporation Limited v. British Columbia Electric Company Limited* , (1962) S.C.R. 642 this Court had to decide whether a receivership order could be made to preserve assets pending a decision as to the constitutionality of certain legislation in British Columbia which litigation would determine whether the Crown had title to the common shares of British Columbia Electric Company Limited which the legislation gave to the Crown.

It was contended that a receivership order could not be made by virtue of the Crown's prerogative of immunity. Chief Justice Kerwin, who delivered the judgement of the Court, said at pp. 644-45;

...In a federal system, where legislative authority is divided, as are also the prerogatives of the Crown, as between the Dominion and the Provinces, it is my view that it is not open to the Crown, either in right of Canada or of a Province, to claim a Crown immunity based upon an interest in certain property, where its very interest in that property depends completely and solely on the validity of the legislation which it has itself passed, if there is a reasonable doubt as to whether such legislation is constitutionally valid. To permit it to do so would be to enable it, by the assertion of rights claimed under legislation which is beyond its powers, to achieve the same results as if the legislation were valid. In a federal system it appears to me that, in such circumstances, the Court has the same jurisdiction to preserve assets whose title is dependent on the validity of the legislation as it has to determine the validity of the legislation itself.

In *The Attorney General of Nova Scotia v. The Attorney General of Canada*, (1951) S.C.R. 31 the Court had to consider the validity of legislation which contemplated a delegation of legislative powers by the provincial Legislature to the Parliament of Canada, and by Parliament to the Provincial Legislature. Chief Justice Rinfret said at p. 34:

> The constitution of Canada does not belong either to Parliament, or to the Legislatures; it belongs to the country and it is there that the citizens of the country will find the protection of the rights to which they are entitled. It is part of that protection that Parliament can legislate only on the subject matters referred to it by section 92. The country is entitled to insist that legislation adopted under section 91 should be passed exclusively by the Parliament of Canada in the same way as the people of each Province are entitled to insist that legislation concerning the matters enumerated in section 92 should come exclusively from their respective Legislatures. In each case the Members elected to Parliament or to the Legislatures are the only ones entrusted with the power and the duty to legislate concerning the subjects exclusively distributed by the constitutional Act to each of them.

> No power of delegation is expressed either in section 91 or in section 92, nor, indeed, is there to be found the power of accepting delegation from one body to the other; and I have no doubt that if it had been the intention to give such powers it would have been expressed in clear and unequivocal language. Under the scheme of the *British North America Act* there were to be, in the words of Lord Atkin in *The Labour Convention Reference* (1937) A.C. 326), 'water-tight compartments which are an essential part of the original structure."

> Neither legislative bodies, federal or provincial, possess any portion of the powers respectively vested in the other and they cannot receive it by delegation. In that connection the word "exclusively" used both in section 91 and in section 92 indicates a settled line of demarcation and it does not belong to either Parliament, or the Legislatures, to confer powers upon the other.

In *Reference re Alberta Statutes*, (1938) S.C.R. 100 the Court considered, *inter alia*, the constitutional validity of *The Accurate News and Information Act* which imposed certain duties of publication upon newspapers published in Alberta. Chief Justice Duff (Davis J. concurring) referred to the right of public discussion and the authority of Parliament to protect that right and said at pp. 133-34:

> ... That authority rests upon the principle that the powers requisite for the protection of the constitution itself arise by necessary implication from *The British North America Act* as a whole *(Fort Frances Pulp & Paper Co. Ltd. v. Manitoba Free Press Co. Ltd.* (1923) A.C. 695); and since the subject-matter in relation to which the power is exercised is not exclusively a provincial matter, it is necessarily vested in Parliament.

It may be noted that the above instances of judicially developed legal principles and doctrines share several char-

77

acteristics. First, none is to be found in express provisions of the *British North America Acts* or other constitutional enactments. Second, all have been perceived to represent constitutional requirements that are derived from the federal character of Canada's constitution. Third, they have been accorded full legal force in the sense of being employed to strike down legislative enactments. Fourth, each was judicially developed in response to a particular legislative initiative in respect of which it might have been observed, as it was by Dickson J. in the *Amax (supra)* case at p. 591, that: "There are no Canadian constitutional law precedents addressed directly to the present issue . . ."

The cases just considered were all decisions of this Court. We have already referred to the judgment of the Privy Council in the *Labour Conventions* case, which, in our opinion, by analogy, is of considerable assistance in determining the issue before the Court. In that case, the Attorney General of Canada argued that the federal government's power to enter into treaties on behalf of a sovereign Canada enabled the Federal Parliament to legislate pursuant to any treaty obligation. That submission was rejected by the Privy Council which held that the Federal Parliament did not derive further legislative competence because of the accession by Canada to sovereign status. The Federal Parliament was not clothed with additional legislative authority in consequence of the commitments it had made under an international treaty.

The contention of the Attorney General of Canada in the present proceedings is that only the Federal Parliament can speak for Canada as a sovereign state. It is the Houses of Parliament which, alone, under the practice developed in the obtaining of amendments to the B.N.A. Act, can submit a request to the Imperial Parliament to amend the B.N.A. Act, and the Imperial Parliament by a firm and unbending convention must comply with such a request. There is therefore, it is contended, nothing which lawfully precludes the submission to the Imperial Parliament by resolution of both Houses of a request for an amendment to the B.N.A. Act which affects the basic division of legislative powers enshrined in the B.N.A. Act.

In our opinion the accession of Canada to sovereign international status did not enable the Federal Parliament, whose legislative authority is limited to the matters defined in s. 91 of the B.N.A. Act unilaterally by means of a resolution of its two Houses, to effect an amendment to the B.N.A. Act which would offend against the basic principle of the division of powers created by that Act. The assertion of such a right, which has never before been attempted, is not only contrary to the federal system created by the B.N.A. Act, but also runs counter to the objective sought to be achieved by s. 7 of the Statute of Westminster.

The federal position in these appeals can be summarized in these terms. While the Federal Parliament lacks legal authority to achieve the objectives set out in the Resolution by the enactment of its own legislation, that limitation upon its authority can be evaded by having the legislation enacted by the Imperial Parliament at the behest of a resolution of the two Houses of the Federal Parliament. This is an attempt by the Federal Parliament to accomplish indirectly that which it is legally precluded from doing directly by perverting the recognized resolution method of obtaining constitutional amendments by the Imperial Parliament for an improper purpose. In our opinion, since it is beyond the power of the Federal Parliament to enact such an amendment, it is equally beyond the power of its two Houses to effect such an amendment through the agency of the Imperial Parliament.

We would adopt the views expressed by the Right Honourable Louis St. Laurent, then Prime Minister of Canada, on January 31, 1949, when in the debate on the address he said:

> With respect to all matters given by the constitution to the provincial governments, nothing this House could do could take anything away from them. We have no jurisdiction over what has been assigned exclusively to the provinces. We cannot ask that what is not within our jurisdiction be changed. We have jurisdiction over the matters assigned to us and we can ask that the manner of dealing with those matters be changed.
> (House of Commons Debates, 1949, vol. 1, at p. 85).

This passage clearly defines the scope of the power of the Federal Parliament to request, on its own motion, amendments to the B.N.A. Act. It is limited to matters which are assigned to the Federal Parliament by the B.N.A. Act.

CONCLUSIONS:

The B.N.A. Act created a federal union. It was of the very essence of the federal nature of the Constitution that the Parliament of Canada and the Provincial Legislatures should have distinct and separate legislative powers. The nature of the legislative powers of the Provinces under s. 92 and the status of the Provincial Legislatures was declared by the Privy Council in the *Hodge (supra)* case and in the *Maritime Bank (supra)* case. We repeat the statement of Lord Watson in the latter case at p. 442:

. . .The object of the Act was neither to weld the provinces into one, nor to subordinate provincial governments to a central authority, but to create a federal government in which they should all be represented, entrusted with the exclusive administration of affairs in which they had a common interest, each province retaining its independence and autonomy.

The continuation of that basic division of legislative powers was recognized in subs. 7(3) of the Statute of Westminster. The Parliament of Canada has no power to trespass on the area of legislative powers given to the Provincial Legislatures. Section 7 of the Statute was intended to safeguard Provincial legislative powers from possible encroachment by the Federal Parliament as a result of the powers being conferred upon the Parliament of Canada by the Statute.

The fact that the status of Canada became recognized as a sovereign state did not alter its federal nature. It is a sovereign state, but its government is federal in character with a clear division of legislative powers. The Resolution at issue in these appeals could only be an effective expression of Canadian sovereignty if it had the support of both levels of government.

The two Houses of the Canadian Parliament claim the power unilaterally to effect an amendment to the B.N.A. Act which they desire, including the curtailment of Provincial legislative powers. This strikes at the basis of the whole federal system. It asserts a right by one part of the Canadian governmental system to curtail, without agreement, the powers of the other part.

There is no statutory basis for the exercise of such a power. On the contrary, the powers of the Senate and the House of Commons, given to them by paragraph 4(a) of the *Senate and House of Commons Act*, excluded the power to do anything inconsistent with the B.N.A. Act. The exercise of such a power has no support in constitutional convention. The constitutional convention is entirely to the contrary. We see no other basis for the recognition of the existence of such a power. This being so, it is the proper function of this Court, in its role of protecting and preserving the Canadian Constitution, to declare that no such power exists. We are, therefore, of the opinion that the Canadian Constitution does not empower the Senate and the House of Commons to cause the Canadian Constitution to be amended in respect of Provincial legislative powers without the consent of the Provinces.

Question B in the Quebec Reference raises the issue as to the power of the Senate and the House of Commons of Canada to cause the Canadian Constitution to be amended "without the consent of the provinces and in spite of the objection of several of them". The Attorney General of Saskatchewan when dealing with Question 3 in the Manitoba and Newfoundland References submitted that it was not necessary in these proceedings for the Court to pronounce on the necessity for the unanimous consent of all the Provinces to the constitutional amendments proposed in the Resolution. It was sufficient, in order to answer the Question, to note the opposition of eight of the provinces which contained a majority of the population of Canada.

We would answer Question B in the negative. We would answer Question 3 of the Manitoba and Newfoundland References in the affirmative without deciding, at this time, whether the agreement referred to in that Question must be unanimous.

3 CONSTITUTIONAL CONVENTION: THE MAJORITY DECISION

BY JUDGES MARTLAND, RITCHIE, DICKSON, BEETZ, CHOUINARD AND LAMER

IN THE MATTER of an Act for expediting the decision of constitutional and other provincial questions, being R.S.M. 1970, c. C-180

AND IN THE MATTER of a Reference pursuant thereto by the Lieutenant Governor in Council to the Court of Appeal for Manitoba for hearing and consideration, the questions concerning the amendment of the Constitution of Canada as set out in Order in Council No. 1020⅓0

THE ATTORNEY GENERAL OF MANITOBA
(Appellant)

—and—

THE ATTORNEY GENERAL OF QUEBEC
THE ATTORNEY GENERAL OF NOVA SCOTIA
THE ATTORNEY GENERAL OF BRITISH COLUMBIA
THE ATTORNEY GENERAL OF PRINCE EDWARD IS-
LAND
THE ATTORNEY GENERAL OF SASKATCHEWAN
THE ATTORNEY GENERAL OF ALBERTA
THE ATTORNEY GENERAL OF NEWFOUNDLAND
FOUR NATIONS CONFEDERACY INC.
(Intervenors)

—v—

THE ATTORNEY GENERAL OF CANADA
(Respondent)

—and—

THE ATTORNEY GENERAL OF ONTARIO
THE ATTORNEY GENERAL OF NEW BRUNSWICK
(Intervenors)

IN THE MATTER of Section 6 or the Judicature Act, R.S.N. 1970, c. 187 as amended,

AND IN THE MATTER OF a Reference by the Lieutenant-Governor in Council concerning the effect and validity of the amendments to the Constitution of Canada sought in the 'Proposed Resolution for a Joint Address to Her Majesty The Queen respecting the Constitution of Canada.''

THE ATTORNEY GENERAL OF CANADA
(Appellant)

—and—

THE ATTORNEY GENERAL OF ONTARIO
THE ATTORNEY GENERAL OF NEW BRUNSWICK
(Intervenors)

—v—

THE ATTORNEY GENERAL OF NEWFOUNDLAND
(Respondent)

—and—

THE ATTORNEY GENERAL OF QUEBEC
THE ATTORNEY GENERAL OF NOVA SCOTIA
THE ATTORNEY GENERAL OF MANITOBA
THE ATTORNEY GENERAL OF BRITISH COLUMBIA
THE ATTORNEY GENERAL OF PRINCE EDWARD IS-
LAND
THE ATTORNEY GENERAL OF SASKATCHEWAN
THE ATTORNEY GENERAL OF ALBERTA
FOUR NATIONS CONFEDERACY INC.
(Intervenors)

83

AND IN THE MATTER of a Reference to the Court of Appeal of Quebec relative to a draft Resolution containing a joint address to Her Majesty The Queen concerning the Constitution of Canada

THE ATTORNEY GENERAL OF QUEBEC

(Appellant

—and—

THE ATTORNEY GENERAL OF CANADA

(Respondent

—and—

THE ATTORNEY GENERAL FOR MANITOBA
THE ATTORNEY GENERAL OF BRITISH COLUMBIA
THE ATTORNEY GENERAL OF PRINCE EDWARD ISLAND
THE ATTORNEY GENERAL OF ALBERTA
THE ATTORNEY GENERAL OF NOVA SCOTIA
THE ATTORNEY GENERAL OF SASKATCHEWAN
FOUR NATIONS CONFEDERACY INC.
(Intervenors supporting the Attorney General of Quebec)

—and—

THE ATTORNEY GENERAL OF ONTARIO
THE ATTORNEY GENERAL OF NEW BRUNSWICK
(Intervenors supporting the Attorney General of Canada)

CORAM:

The Chief Justice and Martland, Ritchie, Dickson, Beetz, Estey, McIntyre, Chouinard and Lamer JJ.

MARTLAND, RITCHIE, DICKSON, BEETZ, CHOUINARD and LAMER JJ.:

The second question in the Manitoba Reference(**Reference re Amendment of the Constitution of Canada (1981) 117 D.L.R. (3d))** and Newfoundland Reference **ibid, 118 D.L.R. 118 (3d)) is the same:**

2. Is it a constitutional convention that the House of Commons and Senate of Canada will not request Her Majesty the Queen to lay before the Parliament of the United Kingdom of Great Britain and Northern Ireland a measure to amend the Constitution of Canada affecting federal-provincial relationships or the powers, rights or privileges granted or secured by the Constitution of Canada to the provinces, their legislatures or governments without first obtaining the agreement of the provinces?

As for question B in the Quebec Reference, it reads in part as follows: *(Translation)*

B. Does the Canadian Constitution empower . . . by . . . convention . . . the Senate and the House of Commons of Canada to cause the Canadian Constitution to be amended without the consent of the provinces and in spite of the objection of several of them, in such a manner as to affect:

(i) the legislative competence of the provincial legislatures in virtue of the Canadian Constitution?

(ii) the status or role of the provincial legislatures or governments within the Canadian Federation?

In these questions, the phrases "Constitution of Canada" and 'Canadian Constitution" do not refer to matters of interest only to the federal government or federal juristic unit. They are clearly meant in a broader sense and embrace the global system of rules and principles which govern the exercise of constitutional authority in the whole and in every part of the Canadian State. They will be used in the same broad sense of these reasons.

The meaning of the second question in the Manitoba and Newfoundland References calls for further observations.

As will be seen later, Counsel for several provinces strenuously argued that the convention exists and requires the agreement of all the provinces. However, we did not understand any of them to have taken the position that the second question in the Manitoba and Newfoundland References should be dealt with and answered as if the last part of the question read

. . .without obtaining the agreement of all the provinces?

Be that as it may, the question should not in our view be so read.

It would have been easy to insert the word "all" into the question had it been intended to narrow its meaning. But we do not think it was so intended. The issue raised by the question is essentially whether there is a constitutional convention that the House of Commons and Senate of Canada will not proceed alone. The thrust of the question is accordingly on whether or not there is a conventional requirement for provincial agreement, not on whether the agreement should be unanimous assuming that it is required. Furthermore, this manner of reading the question is more in keeping with the wording of question B in the Quebec Reference which refers to something less than unanimity when it says:

...without the consent of the provinces and in spite of the objection of several of them. . .

If the questions are thought to be ambiguous, this Court should not, in a constitutional reference, be in a worse position than that of a witness in a trial and feel compelled simply to answer Yes or No. Should it find that a question might be misleading, or should it simply wish to avoid the risk of misunderstanding, the Court is free either to interpret the question as in *Re: Authority of Parliament in relation to the Upper House* (the *Senate Reference*)**(1980) 1 S.C.R. 54 at p. 59**, or it may qualify both the question and the answer as in *Reference re Waters and Water Powers* **(1929) S.C.R. 200**.

I

The nature of constitutional conventions

A substantial part of the rules of the Canadan Constitution are written. They are contained not in a single document called a Constitution but in a great variety of statutes some of which have been enacted by the Parliament of Westminster, such as the *British North America Act 1867* **(ref. 1867, 30 Vict. c. 3.)** (the *B.N.A. Act*) or by the Parliament of Canada, such as *The Alberta Act* **(ref. 1905, 4-5 Edw. VII, c. 3.)**, *The Saskatchewan Act* **(ref. 1905, 4-5 Edw. VII, c. 42.)**, the *Senate and House of Commons Act* **(ref. 1970, R.S.C. c. S-8.)**, or by the provincial legislatures, such as the provincial electoral acts. They are also to be found in orders in council like the Imperial Order in Council of May 16, 1871 admitting British Columbia into the Union, and the Imperial Order in Council of June 26, 1873, admitting Prince Edward Island into the Union.

Another part of the Constitution of Canada consists of the rules of the common law. These are rules which the courts have developed over the centuries in the discharge of their judicial duties. An important portion of these rules concerns the prerogative of the Crown. Sections 9 and 15 of the *B.N.A. Act* provide:

9. The Executive Government and authority of and over Canada is hereby declared to continue and be vested in the Queen.

15. The Commander-in-Chief of the land and Naval Militia, and of all Naval and Military Forces, of and in Canada, is hereby declared to continue and be vested in the Queen.

But the Act does not otherwise say very much with respect to the elements of "Executive Government and authority" and one must look at the common law to find out what they are, apart from authority delegated to the Executive by statute.

The common law provides that the authority of the Crown includes for instance the prerogative of mercy or clemency(ref. **Reference as to the effect of the exercise of the royal prerogative of mercy upon deportation proceedings (1933) S.C.R. 269.**) and the power to incorporate by charter so as to confer a general capacity analogous to that of a natural person.(ref. **Bonanza Creek Gold Mining Company Limited v. Rex (1916) 1 A.C. 566.**) The royal prerogative puts the Crown in a preferred position as a creditor (ref. **Liquidators of the Maritime Bank of Canada v. Receiver General of New Brunswick (1892) A.C. 437.**) or with respect to the inheritance of lands for defect of heirs(ref. **Attorney General of Ontario v. Mercer (1882-83) 8 App. Cas. 767.**) or in relation to the ownership of precious metals(ref. **Attorney General of British Columbia v. Attorney General of Canada (1889) 14 A.C. 295.**) and *bona vacantia.* (ref. **Rex v. Attorney General of British Columbia (1924) A.C. 213.**) It is also under the prerogative and the common law that the

Crown appoints and receives ambassadors, declares war, concludes treaties and it is in the name of the Queen that passports are issued.

Those parts of the Constitution of Canada which are composed of statutory rules and common law rules are generically referred to as the law of the Constitution. In cases of doubt or dispute, it is the function of the courts to declare what the law is and since the law is sometimes breached, it is generally the function of the courts to ascertain whether it has in fact been breached in specific instances and, if so, to apply such sanctions as are contemplated by the law, whether they be punitive sanctions or civil sanctions such as a declaration of nullity. Thus, when a federal or a provincial statute is found by the courts to be in excess of the legislative competence of the legislature which has enacted it, it is declared null and void and the courts refuse to give effect to it. In this sense it can be said that the law of the Constitution is administered or enforced by the courts.

But many Canadians would perhaps be surprised to learn that important parts of the Constitution of Canada, with which they are the most familiar because they are directly involved when they exercise their right to vote at federal and provincial elections, are nowhere to be found in the law of the Constitution. For instance it is a fundamental requirement of the Constitution that if the Opposition obtains the majority at the polls, the Government must tender its resignation forthwith. But fundamental as it is, this requirement of the Constitution does not form part of the law of the Constitution.

It is also a constitutional requirement that the person who is appointed Prime Minister or Premier by the Crown and who is the effective head of the government should have the support of the elected branch of the legislature; in practice this means in most cases the leader of the political party which has won a majority of seats at a general election. Other ministers are appointed by the Crown on the advice of the Prime Minister or Premier when he forms or reshuffles his cabinet. Ministers must continuously have the confidence of the elected branch of the legislature, individually and collectively. Should they lose it, they must either resign or ask the Crown for a dissolution of the legislature and the holding of a general election. Most of the powers of the Crown under the prerogative are exercised only upon the advice of the Prime Minister or the Cabinet which means that they are effectively exercised by the latter, together with the innumerable statutory powers delegated to the Crown in council.

Yet none of these essential rules of the Constitution can be said to be a law of the Constitution. It was apparently Dicey who, in the first edition of his *Law of the Constitution*, in 1885, called them "the conventions of the constitution," (ref. W.S. Holdsworth, The conventions of the eighteenth century constitution, (1932) 17 Iowa Law Rev. 161.) an expression which quickly became current. What Dicey described under these terms are the principles and rules of responsible government, several of which are stated above and which regulate the relations between the Crown, the Prime Minister, the Cabinet and the two Houses of Parliament. These rules developed in Great Britain by way of custom and precedent during the nineteenth century and were exported to such British colonies as were granted self-government.

Dicey first gave the impression that constitutional conventions are a peculiarly British and modern phenomenon. But he recognized in later editions that different conventions are found in other constitutions. As Sir William Holdsworth wrote:

In fact conventions must grow up at all times and in all places where the powers of government are vested in different persons or bodies — where in other words there is a mixed constitution. "The constituent parts of a state," said Burke, (French Revolution, 28) "are we obliged to hold their public faith with each other, and with all those who derive any serious interest under their engagements, as much as the whole state is bound to keep its faith with separate communities." Necessarily conventional rules spring up to regulate the working of the various parts of the constitution, their relations to one another, and to the subject. (ref. W.S. Holdsworth, *op.cit. p. 162.*)

Within the British Empire, powers of government were vested in different bodies which provided a fertile ground for the growth of new constitutional conventions unknown to Dicey whereby self-governing colonies acquired equal and independent status within the Commonwealth. Many of these culminated in the *Statute of Westminster, 1931.* (Ref. 22 Geo. V c.4.)

A federal constitution provides for the distribution of powers between various legislatures and governments and may also constitute a fertile ground for the growth of constitutional conventions between those legislatures and governments. It is conceivable for instance that usage and practice might give birth to conventions in Canada relating to the holding of federal-provincial conferences, the appointment of lieutenant-governors, the reservation and disallowance of provincial legislation. It was to this possibility that Duff C.J.C. alluded when he referred to "constitutional usage or constitutional practice" in *Reference re The Power of the Governor General in Council to disallow provincial legislation and the Power of Reservation of the Lieutenant-Governor of a Province.*(1938) **S.C.R. 71 at p. 78.**) He had previously called them "recognized constitutional conventions" in *Wilson v. Esquimalt and Nanaimo Ry. Co.* **(1922) 1 A.C. 202 at p. 210.**)

The main purpose of constitutional conventions is to ensure that the legal framework of the Constitution will be operated in accordance with the prevailing constitutional values or principles of the period. For example, the constitutional value which is the pivot of the conventions stated above and relating to responsible government is the democratic principle: the powers of the state must be exercised in accordance with the wishes of the electorate; and the constitutional value or principle which anchors the conventions regulating the relationship between the members of the Commonwealth is the independence of the former British colonies.

Being based on custom and precedent, constitutional conventions are usually unwritten rules. Some of them however may be reduced to writing and expressed in the proceedings and documents of imperial conferences, or in the preamble of statutes such as the Statute of Westminster, 1931, or in the proceedings and documents of federal provincial conferences. They are often referred to and recognized in statements made by members of governments.

The conventional rules of the Constitution present one striking peculiarity. In contradistinction to the laws of the Constitution, they are not enforced by the courts. One reason for this situation is that, unlike common law rules, conventions are not judge-made rules. They are not based on judicial precedents but on precedents established by the institutions of government themselves. Nor are they in the nature of statutory commands which it is the function and duty of the courts to obey and enforce. Furthermore, to enforce them would mean to administer some formal sanction when they are breached. But the legal system from which they are distinct does not contemplate formal sanctions for their breach.

Perhaps the main reason why conventional rules cannot be enforced by the courts is that they are generally in conflict with the legal rules which they postulate and the courts are bound to enforce the legal rules. The conflict is not of a type which would entail the commission of any illegality. It results from the fact that legal rules create wide powers, discretions and rights which conventions prescribe should be exercised only in a certain limited manner, if at all.

Some examples will illustrate this point.

As a matter of law, the Queen, or the Governor General or the Lieuttenant-Governor could refuse assent to every bill passed by both Houses of Parliament or by a Legislative Assembly as the case may be. But by convention they cannot of their own motion refuse to assent to any such bill on any ground, for instance because they disapprove of the policy of the bill. We have here a conflict between a legal rule which creates a complete discretion and a conventional rule which completely neutralizes it. But conventions, like laws, are sometimes violated. And if this particular convention were violated and assent were improperly withheld; the courts would be bound to enforce the law, not the convention. They would refuse to enforce the law, not the convention. They would refuse to recognize the validity of a vetoed bill. This is what happened in *Gallant v. The King*,(1949) 2 D.L.R. 425; (1949) 23 M.P.R. 48: See also for a comment on the situation by K.M. Martin in (1946) 24 Can. Bar Rev.

434.), a case in keeping with the classic case of *Stockdale v. Hansard* (1839) 9 ASd. and E. 1, where the English Court of Queen's Bench held that only the Queen and both Houses of Parliament could make or unmake laws. The Lieutenant-Governor who had withheld assent in *Gallant* apparently did so towards the end of his term of office. Had it been otherwise; it is not inconceivable that his withholding of assent might have produced a political crisis leading to his removal from office which shows that if the remedy for a breach of a convention does not lie with the courts, still the breach is not necessarily without a remedy. The remedy lies with some other institutions of government; furthermore it is not a formal remedy and it may be administered with less certainty or regularity than it would be by a court.

Another example of the conflict between law and convention is provided by a fundamental convention already stated above: if after a general election where the Opposition obtained the majority at the polls the Government refused to resign and clung to office, it would thereby commit a fundamental breach of conventions, one so serious indeed that it could be regarded as tantamount to a coup d'etat. The remedy in this case would lie with the Governor General or the Lieutenant-Gooverner as the case might be who would be justified in dismissing the Ministry and in calling on the Opposition to form the Government. But should the Crown be slow in taking this course, there is nothing the courts could do about it except at the risk of creating a state of legal discontinuity, that is a form of revolution. An order or a regulation passed by a Minister under statutory authority and otherwise valid could not be invalidated on the ground that, by convention, the Minister ought no longer to be a Minister. A writ of *quo waranto* aimed at Ministers, assuming that *quo warranto* lies against a Minister of the Crown, which is very doubtful, would be of no avail to remove them from office. Required to say by what warrant they occupy their ministerial office, they would answer that they occupy it by the pleasure of the Crown under a commission issued by the Crown and this answer would be a complete one at law for at law, the Government is in office by the pleasure of the Crown although by convention it is there by the will of the people.

This conflict between convention and law which prevents the courts from enforcing conventions also prevents conventions from crystallizing into laws, unless it be by statutory adoption.

It is because the sanctions of convention rest with institutions of government other than courts, such as the Governor General or the Lieutenant-Governor, or the Houses of Parliament, or with public opinion and ultimately, with the electorate that it is generally said that they are political.

We respectfully adopt the definition of a convention given by the learned Chief Justice of Manitoba, Freedman C.J.M. in the Manitoba Reference at pp. 13 and 14:

> What is a constitutional convention? There is a fairly lengthy literature on the subject. Although there may be shades of difference among the constitutional lawyers, political scientists, and judges who have contributed to that literature, the essential features of a convention may be set forth with some degree of confidence. Thus there is general agreement that a convention occupies a position somewhere in between a usage or custom on the one hand and a constitutional law on the other. There is general agreement that if one sought to fix that position with greater precision he would place convention nearer to law than to usage or custom. There is also general agreement that "a convention is a rule which is regarded as obligatory by the officials to whom it applies." Hogg, "Constitutional Law of Canada," (1977), P. 9. There is, if not general agreement, at least weighty authority, that the sanction for breach of a convention will be political rather than legal.

It should be borne in mind however that, while they are not laws, some conventions may be more important than some laws. Their importance depends on that of the value or principle which they are meant to safeguard. Also they form an integral part of the Constitution and of the constitutional system. They come within the meaning of the word "Constitution" in the preamble of the *British North America Act*, 1867:

> Whereas the Provinces of Canada, Nova Scotia and New Brunswick have expressed their Desire to be federally united .. with a Constitution similar in principle to that of the United Kingdom:

That is why it is perfectly appropriate to say that to violate a convention is to do something which is unconstitutional although it entails no direct legal consequence. But the words "constitutional" and "unconstitutional" may also be used in a strict legal sense, for instance with respect to a statute which is found *ultra vires* or unconstitutional. The

93

foregoing may perhaps be summarized in an equations:
constitutional conventions plus constitutional law equal the
total Constitution of the country.

II
Whether the question should be answered

It was submitted by counsel for Canada and for Ontario
that the second question in the Manitoba and Newfoundland
Reference and the conventional part of question B in the
Quebec Reference ought not to be answered because they do
not raise a justiciable issue and are accordingly not appropriate for a court. It was contended that the issue whether a
particular convention exists or not is a purely political one.
The existence of a definite convention is always unclear and
a matter of debate. Furthermore conventions are flexible,
somewhat imprecise and unsuitable for judicial determination.

The same submission was made in substance to the
three courts below and, in our respectful opinion, rightfully
dismissed by all three of them, Hall J.A. dissenting in the
Manitoba Court of Appeal.

We agree with what Freedman C.J.M. wrote on this
subject in the Manitoba Reference at p. 13:

> In my view this submission goes too far. Its characterization of Ques-
> tion 2 as "purely political" overstates the case. That there is a political ele-
> ment embodied in the question, arising from the contents of the Joint Ad-
> dress, may well be the case. But that does not end the matter. If Qestion 2,
> even if in part political, possesses a constitutional feature, it would legiti-
> mately call for our reply.

> In my view the request for a decision by this Court on whether there is
> a constitutional convention, in the circumstances described, that the Do-
> minion will not act without the agreement of the Provinces poses a ques-
> tion that is, at least in part, constitutional in character. It therefore calls
> for an answer, and I propose to answer it.

Question 2 is not confined to an issue of pure legality but
it has to do with a fundamental issue of constitutionality and
legitimacy. Given the broad statutory basis upon which the
Governments of Manitoba, Newfoundland and Quebec are
empowered to put questions to their three respective Courts
of Appeal, they are in our view entitled to an answer to a
question of this type.

Furthermore, one of the main points made by Manitoba with respect to question 3 was that the constitutional convention referred to in question 2 had become crystallized into a rule of law. Question 3 is admitted to by all to raise a question of law. We agree with Matas J.A. of the Manitoba Court of Appeal that it would be difficult to answer question 3 without an analysis of the points raised in question 2. It is accordingly incumbent on us to answer question 2.

Finally, we are not asked to hold that a convention has in effect repealed a provision of the B.N.A. Act, as was the case in the *Reference re Disallowance (supra)* . Nor are we asked to enforce a convention. We are asked to recognize it if it exists. Courts have done this very thing many times in England and the Commonwealth to provide aid for and background to constitutional or statutory construction. Several such cases are mentioned in the reasons of the majority of this Court relating to the question whether constitutional conventions are capable of crystallizing into law. There are many others, among them:

Commonwealth v. Kreglinger -- *(1925) 37 C.L.R. 393*
Liversidge v. Anderson -- *(1942) A.C. 206*
Carltona Ltd. v. Commissioners of Works -- *(1943) 2 All E.R. 560*
Adegbenro v. Akintola -- *(1963) A.C. 614*
Ibralebbe v. R. -- *(1964) A.C. 900.*

This Court did the same in the recent case of *Arseneau v. The Queen* -- *(1979) 2 S.C.R. 136 at p. 149,* and in the still unreported judgment rendered on April 6, 1981 after the re-hearing of *Attorney General of Quebec v. Peter Blaikie et al* .

In so recognizing conventional rules, the Courts have described them, sometimes commented upon them and given them such precision as is derived from the written form of a judgment. They did not shrink from doing so on account of the political aspects off conventions, nor because of their supposed vagueness, uncertainty or flexibility.

In our view, we should not, in a constitutional reference, decline to accomplish a type of exercise that courts have been doing of their own motion for years.

III

Whether the convention exists

It was submitted by Counsel for Canada, Ontario and New Brunswick that there is no constitutional convention that the House of Commons and Senate of Canada will not request Her Majesty the Queen to lay before the Parliament of Westminster a measure to amend the Constitution of Canada affecting federal-provincial relationships, etc., without first obtaining the agreement of the provinces.

It was submitted by Counsel for Manitoba, Newfoundland, Quebec, Nova Scotia, British Columbia, Prince Edward Island and Alberta that the convention does exist, that it requires the agreement of all the provinces and that the second question in the Manitoba and Newfoundland References should accordingly be answered in the affirmative.

Counsel for Saskatchewan agreed that the question be answered in the affirmative but on a different basis. He submitted that the convention does exist and requires a measure of provincial agreement. Counsel for Saskatchewan further submitted that the resolution before the Court has not received a sufficient measure off provincial consent.

We wish to indicate at the outset that we find ourselves in agreement with the submissions made to this issue by Counsel for Saskatchewan.

1. The class of constitutional amendments contemplated by the question

Constitutional amendments fall into three categories: (1) amendments which may be made by a provincial legislature acting alone under s. 92.1 of the *B.N.A. Act* ; (2) amendments which may be made by the Parliament of Canada acting alone under s. 91.1 of the *B.N.A. Act* ; (3) all other amendments.

The first two categories are irrelevant for the purposes of these References. While the wording of the second and third questions of the Manitoba and Newfoundland References may be broad enough to embrace all amendments in the third category, it is not necessary for us to consider those amendments which affect federal-provincial relationship only indirectly. In a sense, most amendments of the third category are susceptible of affecting federal-provincial relationships to some extent. But we should restrict ourselves to the consideration of amendments which

...directly affect federal-provincial relationships in the sense of changing federal and provincial legislative powers ... (The *Senate Reference* at p. 65.)

The reason for this is that the second and third questions of the Manitoba and Newfoundland References must be read in the light of the first question. They must be meant to contemplate the same specific class of constitutional amendments as the ones which are sought in the "Proposed Resolution for a Joint Address to Her Majesty the Queen respecting the Constitution of Canada." More particularly, they must be meant to address the same type of amendments as the *Charter of Rights* , which abridges federal and provincial legislative powers, and the amending formula, which would provide for the amendment of the Constitution including the distribution of legislative powers.

These proposed amendments present one essential characteristic: they directly affect federal-provincial relationship in changing legislative powers and in providing for a formula to effect such change.

Therefore, in essence although not in terms, the issue raised by the second question in the Manitoba and Newfoundland References is whether there is a constitutional convention for agreement of the provinces to amendments which change legislative powers and provide for a method of effecting such change. The same issue is raised by question B of the Quebec Reference, above quoted in part.

2. Requirements for establishing a convention

The requirements for establishing a convention bear some resemblance with those which apply to customary law. Precedents and usage are necessary but do not suffice. The must be normative. We adopt the following passage of

Sir. W. Ivor Jennings in *The Law and the Constitution* (5th ed. 1959, p. 136.):

We have to ask ourselves three questions: first, what the the precedents; secondly, did the actors in the precedents believe that they were bound by a rule? A single precedent with a good reason may be enough to establish the rule. A whole string of precedents without such a reason will be of no avail, unless it is perfectly certain that the persons concerned regarded them as bound to it.

(i) The precedents

An account of the statutes enacted by the Parliament of Westminster to modify the Constitution of Canada is found in a White Paper published in 1965 under the authority of the Honourable Guy Favreau, then Minister of Justice for Canada, under the title of "The Amendment of the Constitution of Canada" (the *White Paper*). This account is quoted in the *Senate Reference (supra)* but we find in necessary to reproduce it here for convenience:

(1) **The Rupert's Land Act, 1868** authorized the acceptance by Canada of the rights of the Hudson's Bay Company over Rupert's Land and the North-Western Territory. It also provided that, on Address from the Houses of Parliament of Canada, the Crown could declare this territory part of Canada and the Parliament of Canada could make laws for its peace, order and good government.

(1) *The British North America Act* of 1871 ratified the Manitoba Act passed by the Parliament of Canada in 1870, creating the province of Manitoba and giving it a provincial constitution similar to those off the other provinces. The British North America Act of 1871 also empowered the Parliament of Canada to establish new provinces out of any Canadian territory not then included in a province; (but not thereafter to amend such constituting enactment); to alter the boundaries of any province (with the consent of its legislature), and to provide for the administration, peace and good government of any territory not included in a province.

(3) The *Parliament of Canada Act* of 1875 amended section 18 of the British North America Act, 1867, which set forth the privileges, immunities and powers of each of the Houses of Parliament.

(4) The *British North America Act* of 1886 authorized the Parliament of Canada to provide for the representation in the Senate and the House of Commons of any territories not included in any province.

(5) The *Statute Law Revision Act*, 1893 repealed some obsolete provisions of the British America Act of 1867.

(6) The *Canadian Speaker (Appointment of Deputy) Act*, 1895 confirmed an Act of the Parliament of Canada which provided for the appointment of Deputy-Speaker for the Senate.

(7) The *British North America Act*, 1907 established a new scale of financial subsidies to the provinces in lieu of those set forth in section 118 of the British North America Act of 1867. While not expressly repealing the original section, it made its provisions obsolete.

(8) The *British North America Act*, 1915 redefined the Senatorial Divisions of Canada to take into account the provinces of Manitoba, British Columbia, Saskatchewan and Alberta. Although this statute did not expressly amend the text of the original section 22, it did alter its effect.

(9) The *British North America Act*, 1916 provided for the extension of the life of the current Parliament of Canada beyond the normal period of five years.

(10) The *Statute Law Revision Act*, 1927 repealed additional spent or obsolete provisions in the United Kingdom statutes, including two provisions of the British North America Acts.

(11) The *British North America Act*, 1930 confirmed the natural resources agreements between the Government of Canada and the Governments of Manitoba, British Columbia, Alberta and Saskatchewan, giving the agreements the force of law notwithstanding anything in the British North America Acts.

(12) The *Statute of Westminster*, 1931 while not directly amending the British North America Acts, did alter some of their provisions. Thus, the Parliament of Canada was given the power to make laws having extraterritorial effect. Also, Parliament and the provincial legislatures were given the authority, within their powers under the British North America Acts, to repeal any United Kingdom statute that formed part of the law of Canada. This authority, however, expressly excluded the British North America Act itself.

(13) The *British North America Act*, 1940 gave the Parliament of Canada the exclusive jurisdiction to make laws in relation to Unemployment Insurance.

(14) The *British North America Act*, 1943 provided for the postponement of redistribution of the seats in the House of Commons until the first session of Parliament after the cessation of hostilities.

(15) The *British North America Act*, 1946 replaced section 51 of the British North America Act, 1867, and altered the provisions for the readjustment of representation in the House of Commons.

(16) The *British North America Act*, 1949 confirmed the Terms of Union between Canada and Newfoundland.

(17) The *British North America Act (No. 2)*, 1949 gave the Parliament of Canada authority to amend the Constitution of Canada with certain exceptions.

(18) The *Statute Law Revision Act*, 1950 repealed an obsolete section of the British North America Act, 1867.

(19) The *British North America Act*, 1951 gave the Parliament of Canada concurrent jurisdiction with the provinces to make laws in relation to Old Age Pensions.

(20) The *British North America Act*, 1960 amended section 99 and altered the tenure of office of superior court judges.

(21) The *British North America Act*, 1964 amended the authority conferred upon the Parliament of Canada by the British North America Act, 1951, in relation to benefits supplementary to Old Age Pensions.

(22) *Amendment by Order in Council* Section 146 of the British North America Act, 1867 provided for the admission of other British North American territories by Order in Council and stipulated that the provisions of any such Order in Council would have the same effect as if enacted by the

Parliament of the United Kingdom. Under this section, Rupert's Land and North-Western Territory were admitted by Order in Council on June 23rd, 1870; British Columbia by Order in Council on May 16th, 1871; Prince Edward Island by Oder in Council on June 26th, 1873. Because all of these Orders in Council contained provisions of a constitutional character — adapting the provisions of the British North America Act to the new provinces, but with some modifications in each case — they may therefore be regarded as constitutional amendments.

(The amendments appear to have been done by the Parliament of Westminster on its own initiative and not in response to a joint resolution of the Senate and House of Commons).

For reasons already stated, these precedents must be considered selectively. They must also be considered in positive as well as in negative terms.

Of these twenty-two amendments or groups of amendments, five directly affected federal-provincial relationships in the sense of changing provincial legislative powers: they are the amendment of 1930, the *Statute of Westminster*, *1931*, and the amendments of 1940, 1951 and 1964.

Under the agreements confirmed by the 1930 amendment, the Western provinces were granted ownership and administrative control of their natural resources so as to place these provinces in the same position vis-a-vis natural resources as the original confederating colonies. The Western provinces, however, received these natural resources subject to some limits on their power to make laws relating to hunting and fishing rights of Indians. Furthermore, the agreements did provide a very substantial object for the provincial power to make laws relating to "The Management and Sale of Public Lands belonging to the Province and of the Timber and Wood thereon" under s. 92.5 of the *B.N.A. Act.* The long title reads as follows:

An Act to confirm and give effect to certain agreements entered into between the Government of the Dominion of Canada and the Government of the Provinces of Manitoba, British Columbia, Alberta and Saskatchewan respectively

The preamble of the Act recites that "each of the said agreements has been duly approved by the Parliament of Canada and by the Legislature of the Province to which it relates." The other provinces lost no power, right or privilege in consequence. In any event, the proposed transfer of natural resources to the Western provinces had been discussed at the Dominion-Provincial Conference and had

met with general approval: **Paul Gerin-Lajoie,** *Constitu-*
tional Amendment in Canada. **(ref. 1950, University of To-**
ronto Press, pp.91 and 92.)

All the provinces agreed to the passing of the *Statue of*
Westminster, 1931. It changed legislative powers: Parliament and the Legislatures were given the authority, within
their powers, to repeal any United Kingdom statute that
formed part of the law of Canada; Parliament was also
given the power to make laws having extra-territorial effect.

The 1940 amendment is of special interest in that it
transferred an exclusive legislative power from the provincial Legislatures to the Parliament of Canada.

In 1938, the Speech from the Throne stated:

The co-operation of the provinces has been sought with a view to an
amendment of the British North America Act, which would empower the
parliament of Canada to enact forthwith a national scheme of unemployment insurance. My ministers hope the proposal may meet with early approval, in order that unemployment insurance legislation may be enacted
during the present session of pariliament. (ref. Commons Debates, 1938,
p.2.)

In November 1937, the Government of Canada had
communicated with the provinces and asked for their views
in principle. A draft amendment was later circulated. By
March 1938, five of the nine provinces had approved the
draft amendment. Ontario had agreed in principle, but Alberta, New Brunswick and Quebec declined to join in. The
proposed amendment was not proceeded with until June
1940 when Prime Minister King announced to the House of
Commons that all nine provinces had assented to the proposed amendment.(ref. **Paul Gerin-Lajoie,** *(op. cit.)*
p.106)

The 1951 and 1964 amendments changed the legislative
powers: areas of exclusive provincial competence became
areas of concurrent legislative competence. They were
agreed upon by all the provinces.

These five amendments are the only ones which can be
viewed as positive precedents whereby federal-provincial
relationships were directly affected in the sense of changing
legislative powers.

Every one of these five amendments was agreed upon by each province whose legislative authority was affected.

In negative terms, no amendment changing provincial legislative powers has been made since Confederation when agreement of a province whose legislative powers would have been changed was withheld.

There are no exceptions.

Furthermore, in even more telling negative terms, in 1951, an amendment was proposed to give the provinces a limited power of indirect taxation. Ontario and Quebec did not agree and the amendment was not proceeded with.(**ref. Commons Debates, 1951 pp. 2682 and 2726 to 2743**)

The Constitutional Conference of 1960 devised a formula for the amendment of the Constitution of Canada. Under this formula, the distribution of legislative powers could have been modified. The great majority of the participants found the formula acceptable but some differences remained and the proposed amendment was not proceeded with. (**ref. The _White Paper_, p. 29.**)

In 1964, a conference of first ministers unanimously agreed on an amending formula that would have permitted the modification of legislative powers. Quebec subsequently withdrew its agreement and the proposed amendment was not proceeded with. (**ref. Senate House of Commons Special Joint Committees on Constituation of Canada, issue No. 5, August 23, 1978 p. 14, Professor Lederman.**)

Finally, in 1971, proposed amendments which included an amending formula were agreed upon by the federal government and eight of the ten provincial goverments. Quebec disagreed and Saskatchewan which had a new government did not take a position because it was believed the disagreement of Quebec rendered the question academic. The proposed amendments were not proceeded with. (**ref. Gerald A. Beaudoin, _Le partage des pouvoirs_, Editions de l'Universite d'Ottawa, Ottawa, 1980 p. 349.**)

The accumulation of these precedents, positive and negative, concurrent and without exception, does not of itself suffice in establishing the existence of the convention; but it unmistakedly points in its direction. Indeed, if the precedents stood alone, it might be argued that unanimity is required.

In the *Senate Reference (supra)*, this Court went a considerable distance in recognizing the significance of some of these precedents when it wrote at pages 63 to 65:

> The amendments of 1940, 1951, 1960 and 1964, respecting unemployment insurance, old age pensions, the compulsory retirement of judges and adding supplementary benefits to old age pensions all had the unanimous consent of the provinces.
>
> The apparent intention of the 1949 amendment to the Act which enacted s. 91(1) was to obviate the necessity for the enactment of a statute of the British Parliament to effect amendments to the Act which theretofore had been obtained through a joint resolution of both Houses of Parliament and without provincial consent. Legislation enacted since 1949 pursuant to s. 91(1) has not, to quote the White Paper, "affected federal-provincial relationships." The following statutes have been enacted by the Parliament of Canada.

The Court then enumerated the five amendments enacted by the Parliament of Canada pursuant to s. 91(10 of the *B.N.A. Act* and continuted:

> All of these measures dealt with what might be described as federal "house-keeping" matters which, according to the practice existing before 1949, would have been referred to the British Parliament by way of a joint resolution of both Houses of Parliament, and without the consent of the provinces.

In our respectful opinion, the majority of the Quebec Court of Appeal fell into error on this issue in failing to differentiate between various types of constitutional amendments. The Quebec Court of Appeal put all or practically all constitutional amendments since 1867 on the same footing and, as could then be expected, concluded not only that the convention requiring provincial consent did not exist but that there even appeared to be a convention to the contrary. (See the reasons of Crete, C.J.Q. and Turgeon J.A. at pages 92 and 124 of the case in the Quebec Reference. Owen J.A. agreed with Turgeon J.A. on this issue, and Belanger J.A. with both Crete C.J.O. and Turgeon J.A.).

The Manitoba Court of Appeal was similarly misled, in our respective opinion, but to a lesser extent, which perhaps explains that Freedman C.J.M. wrote at p. 21 of the Manitoba Reference, speaking for himself, Matas and Huband, JJ. A. on this point:

> That we may be moving towards such a convention is certainly a tenable view. But we have not yet arrived there.

We do not think it is necessary to deal with classes of constitutional amendments other than those which change legislative powers or provide for a method to effect such change. But we will briefly comment on two amendments about which much has been made to support the argument against the existence of the convention. These are the amendment of 1907 increasing the scale of financial subsidies to the provinces and the amendment of 1949 confirming the Terms of Union between Canada and Newfoundland.

It was contended that British Columbia objected to the 1907 amendment which had been agreed upon by all the other provinces.

Even if it were so, this precedent would at best constitute an argument against the unanimity rule.

But the fact is that British Columbia did agree in principle with the increase of financial subsidies to the provinces. It wanted more and objected to the proposed finality of the increase. The finality aspect was deleted from the amendment by the United Kingdom authorities. Mr. Winston Churchill, Under Secretary of State for the Colonies made the following comment in the House of Commons:

In deference to the representations of British Columbia the words "final and unalterable" applying to the revised scale, have been omitted from the Bill. (ref. Commons Debates (U.K.) June 13, 1907 p. 1617.)

In the end, the Premier of British Columbia did not refuse to agree to the Act being passed.A.B. Keith, *The Constitutional Law of the British Dominions*, 1933, p. 109.)

With respect to the 1949 amendment, it was observed by Turgeon J. A. in the Quebec Reference that, without Quebec's consent, this amendment confirmed the Quebec-Labrador Boundary as delimited in the report delivered by the Judicial Committee of the Privy Council on March 1, 1927.

The entry of Newfoundland into Confederation was contemplated from the beginning by s. 146 of the B.N.A. Act. It was at the request of Quebec in 1904 that the dispute relating to the boundary was ultimately submitted to the Judicial Committee.(ref. Minute of Privy Council (Canada) P.C. 82 of M. April 18, 1904) Quebec participated in the litigation, being represented by counsel appointed and paid by the Province, although the Province did not intervene separately from Canada. When the 1949 amendment was passed, the Premier of Quebec is reported to have stated at a press conference simply that the Province should have been 'consulted' or 'advised' as a matter of 'courtesy.' He is not reported as having said that the consent of the Province was required. See Luce Patenaude, *Le Labrador a l'heure de la contestation.*(ref. 1972, Presses de l'Universite de Montreal, pages 6, 7, 13, 14, 193 and 194) The Premier of Nova Scotia spoke to the same effect. Neither Premier made any formal demand or protest. (ref. Paul Gerin-Lajoie (op. cit.) p. 129)

We fail to see how this precedent can affect the convention.

It was also observed by Turgeon J. A. in the Quebec Reference that the *Charter of Rights* annexed to the proposed Resolution for a Joint Address does not alter the distribution of powers between the Parliament of Canada and the provincial legislatures.

This observation may be meant as an argument to the effect that the five positive precedents mentioned above should be distinguished and ought not to govern the situation before the Court since in those five cases the distribution of legislative powers was altered.

To this argument we would reply that if provincial consent was required in those five cases, it would be *a fortiori* required in the case at bar.

Each of those five constitutional amendments effected a limited change in legislative powers, affecting one head of legislative competence such as unemployment insurance. Whereas if the proposed *Charter of Rights* became law, every head of provincial (and federal) legislative authority could be affected. Furthermore, the *Charter of Rights* would operate retrospectively as well as prospectively with the result that laws enacted in the future as well as in the past, even before Confederation, would be exposed to attack if inconsistent with the provisions of the *Charter of Rights*. This *Charter* would thus abridge provincial legislative authority on a scale exceeding the effect of any previous constitutional amendment for which provincial consent was sought and obtained.

(ii) The actors treating the rule as binding

In the White Paper, one finds this passage at pages 10 and 11:

PROCEDURES FOLLOWED IN THE PAST
IN SECURING AMENDMENTS TO THE BRITISH
NORTH AMERICA ACT

The procedures for amending a constitution are normally a fundamental part of the laws and conventions by which a country is government. This is particularly true if the constitution is embodied in a formal document as is the case in such federal states as Australia, the United States and Switzerland. In these countries, the amending process forms an important part of their constitutional law.

In this respect, Canada has been in a unique constitutional position. Not only did the British North America Act ot provide for its amendment by Canadian legislative authority, except to the extent outlined at the beginning of this chapter, but it also left Canada without any clearly defined procedure for securing constitutional amendments from the British Parliament. As a result, procedures have varied from time to time, with recurring controversies and doubts over the conditions under which various provisions of the Constitution should be amended.

Certain rules and principles relating to amending procedures have nevertheless developed over the years. They have emerged from the practices and procedures employed in securing various amendments to the British North America Act since 1867. Though not constitutionally binding in any strict sense, they have come to be recognized and accepted in practice as part of the amendment process in Canada.

In order to trace and describe the manner in which these rules and principles have developed, the approaches used to secure amendments through the Parliament of the United Kingdom over the past 97 years are described in the following paragraphs. Not all the amendments are included in this review, but only those that have contributed to the development of accepted constitutional rules and principles.

There follows a list of fourteen constitutional amendments thought to 'have contributed to the development of accepted constitutional rules and principles.' The White Paper then goes on to state these principles, at p. 15:

The first general principle that emerges in the foregoing resume is that although an enactment by the United Kingdom is necessary to amend the British North America Act, such action is taken only upon formal request from Canada. No Act of the United Kingdom Parliament affecting Canada is therefore passed unless it is requested and consented to by Canada. Conversely, every amendment requested by Canada in the past has been enacted.

The second general principle is that the sanction of Parliament is required for a request to the British Parliament for an amendment to the British North America Act. This principle was established early in the history of Canada's constitutional amendments, and has not been violated since 1895. The procedure invariably is to seek amendments by a joint Address of the Canadian House of Commons and Senate to the Crown.

The third general principle is that no amendment to Canada's Constitution will be made by the British Parliament merely upon the request of a Canadian province. A number of attempts to secure such amendments have been made, but none has been successful. The first such attempt was

106

made as early as 1868, by a province which was at that time dissatisfied with the terms of Confederation. This was followed by other attempts in 1869, 1874 and 1887. The British Government refused in all cases to act on provincial government representations on the grounds that it should not intervene in the affairs of Canada except at the request of the federal government representing all of Canada.

The fourth general principle is that the Canadian Parliament will not request an amendment directly affecting federal-provincial relationships without prior consultation and agreement with the provinces. This principle did not emerge as early as others but since 1907, and particularly since 1930, has gained increasing recognition and acceptance. The nature and the degree of provincial participation in the amending process, however, have not lent themselves to easy definition.

The text which precedes the four general principles makes it clear that it deals with conventions. It refers to the laws and conventions by which a country is governed and to constitutional rules which are not binding in any strict sense (that is in a legal sense) but which have come to be recognized and accepted in practice as part of the amendment process in Canada. The first three general principles are statements of well-known constitutional conventions governing the relationships between Canada and the United Kingdom with respect to constitutional amendments.

In our view, the fourth general principle equally and unmistakedly states and recognizes as a rule of the Canadian Constitution the convention referred to in the second question of the Manitoba and Newfoundland References as well as in question B of the Quebec Reference, namely that there is a requirement for provincial agreement to amendments which change provincial legislative powers.

This statement is not a casual utterance. It is contained in a carefully drafted document which had been circulated to all the provinces prior to its publication and been found satisfactory by all of them. (ref. **Commons Debates, 1965, p. 11574. Background paper published by the Government of Canada, *The Role of the United Kingdom in the Amendment of the Canadian Constitution* (March 1981) at p. 30.**) It was published as a White Paper, that is as an official statement of government policy, under the authority of the Federal Minister of Justice as member of a Government responsible to Parliament neither House of which, so far as we know, has taken issue with it. This statement is a recognition by all the actors in the precedents that the requirement of provincial agreement is a constitutional rule.

In the Manitoba Reference, Freedman C.J.M. took the view that the third sentence in the fourth general principle stated in the *White Paper* contradicted, and therefore negated, the first sentence.

With the greatest respect, this interpretation is erroneous. The first sentence is concerned with the existence of the convention, and the third sentence, not with its existence, but with the measure of provincial agreement which is necessary with respect to this class of constitutional amendment. It seems clear that while the precedents taken alone point at unanimity, the unanimity precedents taken alone point at unanimity, the unanimity principle cannot be said to have been accepted by all the actors in the precedents.

This distinction is illustrated by statements made by Prime Minister King in the House of Commons in 1938 and 1940 with respect to the unemployment insurance amendment.

In 1938, some provinces had not yet assented to the unemployment insurance amendment and one finds the following exchange in the Commons Debates:

Right Hon. R. B. BENNETT (Leader of the Opposition): Perhaps the Prime Minister would not object to a supplementary question: Does he conceive it necessary or desirable that all the provinces should agree before action is taken?

Mr. MACKENZIE KING: I do not think this is the moment to answer that question. We had better wait and see what replies we get in the first instance. (ref. Commons Debates, 1938, p. 1747.)

In 1940, Mr. J. T. Thorson, not then a member of the Government, took issue with the contention that it was necessary to obtain the consent of the provinces before an application is made to amend the *B.N.A. Act*. Mr. Lapointe replied:

May I tell my hon. friend that neither the Prime Minister nor I have said it is necessary, but it may be desirable. (ref. Commons Debates, 1940, p. 1122.)

But what the Prime Minister had said in fact was this:

We have avoided anything in the nature of coercion of any of the provinces. Moreover we have avoided the raising of a very critical constitutional

question, namely, whether or not in amending the British North America Act it is absolutely necessary to secure the consent of all the provinces, or whether the consent of a certain number of provinces would of itself be sufficient. That question may come up but not in reference to unemployment insurance at some time later on. (ref. Commons Debates, 1940, p. 1117.)

This statement expressed some uncertainty as to whether unanimity is a necessity, but none as to whether substantial provincial support is required.

As for Mr. Lapointe's reply, it is non-committal and must be qualified by several other statements he made indicating the necessity of provincial consent.9ref. For instance: Commons Debates, 1924, p.520; Commons Debates, 1925, p. 298; Commons Debates, 1940, p. 1110; Commons Debates, 1951, pp. 1477 and 1478)

Prime Minister Bennett had expressed a similar concern with respect to the unanimity rule during the Dominion-Provincial Conference of 1931. He is reported to have said:

As to the requirement of unanimity for change in the British North America Act this would mean that one Province, say Prince Edward Island, might absolutely prevent any change. No state at present required unanimity. Australia does not; nor does South Africa, a bi-lingual country. From one point of view he (Mr. Bennett) could recognize that unanimity might be desirable, but from another it seems to be wholly out of keeping with present political developments in the British Empire and indeed in the world. There must, of course, be safeguards for minorities but there must be no absolute rigidity as regards change. (ref. Report of Dominion-Provincial Conference 1931, pp.8 and 9.)

We were referred to an abundance of declarations made by Canadian politicians on this issue. A few are unfavourable to the provincial position but they were generally made by politicians such as Mr. J.T. Thorson who were not Ministers in office and could not be considered as "actors in the precedents."

Most declarations made by statesmen favour the conventional requirement of provincial consent. We will quote only two such declarations.

In discussing the 1943 amendment, Mr. St. Laurent argued that the amendment did not alter the allocation of federal and provincial powers. He said:

The Honourable L.S. St. Laurent (Minister of Justice) . . . I would readily concede to hon. members that if there were to be any suggested

109

amendment to change the allocation of legislative or administrative jurisdiction as between the provinces, on the one hand, and the federal parliament, on the other, it could not properly be done without the consent of the
organism that was set up by the constitution to have powers that would as-
sumedly be taken from that organism. (. . .)

I submit that it would have been quite improper to take away from
the provinces without their consent anything that they had by the constitution. (ref. Commons Debates, 1943, p. 4366.)

The statement is addressed at constitutional propriety
which is the terminology ordinarily used for conventions.

In 1960, it was suggested to Prime Minister Diefenbaker
that his proposed *Canadian Bill of Rights* be entrenched in
the Constitution and made binding on the provinces as
would be the *Charter of Rights* annexed to the proposed
Resolution for a Joint Address. Here is how he dealt with
this suggestion:

They say, if you want to make this effective it has to cover the provinces too. Any one advocating that must realize the fact that there is no
chance of securing the consent of all the provinces . . .

As far as constitutional amendment is concerned, it is impossible of
attainment at this time.

Mr. Winch: Why?

Mr. Diefenbaker: Simply because of the fact that the consent of the
provinces to any interference with property and civil rights cannot be secured.

I also want to add that if at any time the provinces are prepared to
give their consent to a constitutional amendment embodying a bill of rights
comprising these freedoms, there will be immediate co-operation from this
government. We will forthwith introduce a constitutional amendment cov-
ering not only the federal, but the provincial jurisdictions when and if there
is consent by the provinces everywhere in this country. (ref. Commons Debates, 1960, pp. 5648 and 5649.)

Prime Minister Diefenbaker was clearly of the view
that the *Canadian Bill of Rights* could not be entrenched in
the Constitution and made to apply to the provinces without
the consent of all of them. We have also indicated that while
the precedents point at unanimity, it does not appear that
all the actors in the precedents have accepted the unanimity
rule as a binding one.

In 1965, the White Paper had stated that:

The nature and the degree of provincial participation in the amending process . . . have not lent themselves to easy definition.

Nothing has occured since then which would permit us
to conclue in a more precise manner.

Nor can it be said that this lack of precision is such as
to prevent the principle from acquiring the constitutional

status of a conventional rule. If a consensus had emerged on the measure of provincial agreement, an amending formula would quickly have been enacted and we would not longer be in the realm of conventions. To demand as much precision as if this were the case and as if the rule were a legal one is tantamount to denying that this area of the Canadian Constitution is capable of being governed by conventional rules.

Furthermore, the Government of Canada and the Governments of the provinces have attempted to reach a consensus on a constitutional amending formula in the course of ten federal-provincial conferences held in 1927, 1931, 1935, 1950, 1960, 1964, 1971, 1978, 1979 and 1980. **(ref. Gerald A. Beaudoin,** *op. cit.* **at p. 346.)** A major issue at these conferences was the quantification of provincial consent. No consensus was reached on this issue. But the discussion of this very issue for more than fifty years postulates a clear recognition by all the governments concerned of the principle that a substantial degree of provincial consent is required.

It would not be appropriate for the Court to devise in the abstract a specific formula which would indicate in positive terms what measure of provincial agreement is required for the convention to be complied with. Conventions by their nature develop in the political field and it will be for the political actors, not this Court, to determine the degree of provincial consent required.

It is sufficient for the Court to decide that at least a substantial measure of provincial consent is required and to decide further whether the situation is one where Ontario and New Brunswick agree with the proposed amendments whereas the eight other provinces oppose it. By no conceivable standard could this situation be thought to pass muster. It clearly does not disclose a sufficient measure of provincial agreement. Nothing more should be said about this.

(iii) A reason for the rule

The reason for the rule is the federal principle. Canada is a federal union. The preamble of the *B.N.A. Act* **states that**

the Provinces of Canada, Nova Scotia, and New Brunswick have expressed their Desire to be federally united . . .

The federal character of the Canadian Constitution was recognized in innumerable judicial pronouncements. We will quote only one, that of Lord Watson in *Liquidators of the Maritime Bank of New Brunswick (supra)* at pp. 441, 442:

The object of the Act was neither to weld the provinces into one, nor to subordinate provincial governments to a central authority, but to create a federal government in which they should all be represented, entrusted with the exclusive administration of affairs in which they had a common interest, each province retaining its independence and autonomy.

The federal principle cannot be reconciled with a state of affairs where the modification of provincial legislative powers could be obtained by the unilateral action of the federal authorities. It would indeed offend the federal principal that "a radical change to (the) constitution (be) taken at the request of a bare majority of the members of the Canadian House of Commons and Senate."(**Report of Dominion-Provincial Conference 1931, p. 3.**)

This is an essential requirement of the federal principle which was clearly recognized by the Dominion-Provincial Converence of 1931. This conference had been convened to consider the proposed Statute of Westminister as well as a draft of s. 7 which dealt exclusively with the Canadian position.

At the opening of the Conference, Prime Minister Bennett said:

It should be noted that nothing in the Statute confers on the Parliament of Canada the power to alter the constitution.

The position remained that nothing in the future could be done to amend the British North Americ Act except as the result of appropriate action taken in Canada and in London. In the past such appropriate action had been an address by both Houses of the Canadian Parliament to the Parliament of Westminister. It was recognized, however, that this might result in a radical change to our constitution taken at the request of a bare majority of the members of the Canadian House of Commons and Senate. The original draft of the Statute appeared, in the opinion of some provincial authorities, to sanction such a procedure, but in the draft before the conference this was clearly not the case. (Ref. D-PC 1931, pp3. and 4.)

This did not satisfy Premier Taschereau of Quebec who, the next day, said:

Do we wish the British North America Act to be amended at the request of the Dominion only, without the consent of the Provinces? Do we wish it to be amended by the Parliament of Canada? Quebec could not accept either of these suggestions. She was not prepared to agree that the British North America Act might be amended without the consent of the Provinces. (D-PC 1931, p. 12.)

Mr. Geoffrion, of the Quebec Delegation, suggested an amendment to s. 7(1) of the draft statute, in order to meet the difficulty.

Prime Minister Bennett replied:

> Our purpose is to leave things as they are and we are definitely trying not to do what Mr. Ttaschereau suggests may be done. (D-PC 1931, p. 18.)

The following day, the Conference had before it another draft of s. 7 the first paragraph of which was the one which was ultimately adopted. Premier Taschereau was not yet reassured:

> Mr. Taschereau said that so far as the repeal of the Colonial Laws Validity Act was concerned he had objection to make. Further, the new draft of Section 7 struck him favorably, but more time was necessary for its consideration. However, the Statute, both in its preamble and in Section 4 still, by implication, gave the Dominion the sole right to request an amendment of the British North America Act. It put in black and white what had been the practice of the past. Can we be assured, he asked, that the Government of the Dominion will make no request for an amendment of the British North America Act at Westminster without the consent of the Provinces? (D-PC 1931, p. 18.)

Prime Minister Bennett replied:

> Mr. Bennett felt that Mr. Taschereau's fears concerning the amendment of the constitution by the Dominion action alone were dealt with by Sub-section 1 of the new Section 7. Mr. Taschereau replied that he realized that the power in respect to amendment was not altered by the Statute, but that the practice in that connection had been put down in black nd whites, and that practice, which left out the Provinces, was not satisfactory.
> Mr. Bennett did not feel that the statute went so far. It was his opinion that in minor amendments such as a change in the quorum of the House of Commons there was no reason for consulting the Provinces, but that in more important amendments, such as the distribution of legislative power, the Provinces should be course, be consulted. (D-PC 1931, p. 19.)

> . . .

> Previous amendments to the British North America Act had been noncontroversal, but Mr. Taschereau could assure his colleagues that there would be no amendment to the constitution of Canada in its federal aspect without consulting the Provinces which, it must be remembered had the same powers within their domain that the Dominion has within hers. (D-PC 1931, pp. 19 and 20.)

Several other Premiers shared the concern of Premier Taschereau. It was to meet this concern that s. 7 (1) of the *Statute of Westminister, 1931* was re-drafted. What the re-drafting accomplished as a matter of law is an issue which arises under the third question of the Manitoba and Newfoundland References. But the fact that an attempt was made to do something about it as a matter of law carries all the more weight on the conventional plane.

It is true also that Prime Minister Bennett spoke of consultation of the provinces rather than of their consent but this must be understood in the light of his previously quoted statement expressing his reluctance to accept the unanimity principle.

Furthermore, as was stated in the fourth general principle of the *White Paper* , the requirement of provincial consent did not emerge as early as other principles, but it has gained increasing recognition and acceptance since 1907 and particularly since 1930. This is clearly demonstrated by the proceedings of the Dominion-Provincial Conference of 1931.

Then followed the positive precedents of 1940, 1951 and 1964 as well as the abortive ones of 1951, 1960 and 1964, all discussed above. By 1965, the rule had become recognized as a binding constitutional one formulated in the fourth general principle of the *White Paper* already quoted reading in part as follows:

The *fourth general principal* is that the Canadian Parliament will not request an amendment directly affecting federal-provincial relationships without prior consultation and agreement with the provinces.

The purpose of this conventional rule is to protect the federal character of the Canadian Constitution and prevent the anomaly that the House of Commons and Senate could obtain by simple resolutions what they could not validly accomplish by statute.

It was contended by Counsel for Canada, Ontario and New Brunswick that the proposed amendments would not offend the federal principle and that, if they became law, Canada would remain a federation. The federal principle would even be re-inforced, it was said, since the provinces would as a matter of law be given an important role in the amending formula.

It is true that Canada would remain a federation if the proposed amendments became law. But it would be a different federation made different at the instance of a majority in the Houses of the federal Parliament acting alone. It is this process itself which offends the federal principle.

It was suggested by Counsel for Saskatchewan that the proposed amendments were perhaps severable; that the proposed *Charter of Rights* offended the federal principal in that it would unilaterally alter legislative powers whereas the proposed amending formula did not offend the federal principle.

To this suggestion we cannot accede. Counsel for Canada (as well as Counsel for other parties and all intervenors) took the firm position that the proposed amendment formed an unseverable package. Furthermore, and to repeat, whatever the result, the process offends the federal principle. It was to guard against this process that the constitutional convention came about.

IV

Conclusion

We have reached the conclusion that the agreement of the provinces of Canada, no views being expressed as to its quantification, is constitutionally required for the passing of the "Proposed Resolution for a joint Address to Her Majesty respecting the Constitution of Canada" and that the passing of this Resolution without such agreement would be unconstitutional in the conventional sense.

We would, subject to these reasons, answer question 2 of the Manitoba and Newfoundland References and that part of question B in the Quebec Reference which relates to conventions as follows:

2. Is it a constitutional convention that the House of Commons and Senate of Canada will not request Her Majesty the Queen to lay before the Parliament of the United Kingdom of Great Britain and Northern Ireland a measure to amend the Constitution of Canada affecting federal-provincial relationships or the powers, rights or privileges granted or secured by the Constitution of Canada to the provinces, their legislatures or governments without first obtaining the agreement of the provinces?

YES

(Translation)

1   B. Does the Canadian Constitution empower . . . by . . . convention
. . . the Senate and the House of Commons of Canada to cause the Canadian
Constitution to be amended without the consent of the provinces and in
spite of the objection of several of them, in such a manner as to affect:

(i) the legislative competence of the provincial legislatures in virtue of
the Canadian Constitution?

(ii) the status or role of the provincial legislatures or governments
within the Canadian Federation?

NO

4 CONSTITUTIONAL CONVENTION: THE MINORITY DECISION

BY CHIEF JUSTICE LASKIN AND JUDGES ESTEY AND McINTYRE

IN THE MATTER of an Act for expediting the decision of constitutional and other provincial questions, being R.S.M. 1970, c. C-180

AND IN THE MATTER of a Reference pursuant thereto by the Lieutenant Governor in Council to the Court of Appeal for Manitoba for hearing the consideration, the questions concerning the amendment of the Constitution of Canada as set out in Order in Council No. 1020/80

THE ATTORNEY GENERAL OFF MANITOBA
(Appellant)

—and—

THE ATTORNEY GENERAL OF QUEBEC
THE ATTORNEY GENERAL OF NOVA SCOTIA
THE ATTORNEY GENERAL OF BRITISH COLUMBIA
THE ATTORNEY GENERAL OF PRINCE EDWARD ISLAND
THE ATTORNEY GENERAL OF SASKATCHEWAN
THE ATTORNEY GENERAL OF ALBERTA
THE ATTORNEY GENERAL OF NEWFOUNDLAND
FOUR NATIONS CONFEDERACY INC.
(Intervenors)

v.

THE ATTORNEY GENERAL OF CANADA
(Respondent)

117

—and—

THE ATTORNEY GENERAL OF ONTARIO
THE ATTORNEY GENERAL OF NEW BRUNSWICK
(Intervenors)

IN THE MATTER of Section 6 of The Judicature Act,
R.S.N. 1970, c. 187 as amended,

AND IN THE MATTER OF a Reference by the Lieutenant-Governor in Council concerning the effect and validity
of the amendments to the Constitution of Canada sought in
the "Proposed Resolution for a Joint Address to Her Majesty The Queen respecting the Constitution of Canada"

THE ATTORNEY GENERAL OF CANADA
(Appellant)
—and—

THE ATTORNEY GENERAL OF ONTARIO
THE ATTORNEY GENERAL OF NEW BRUNSWICK
(Intervenors)

v.

THE ATTORNEY GENERAL OF NEWFOUNDLAND
(Respondent)

—and—

THE ATTORNEY GENERAL OF QUEBEC
THE ATTORNEY GENERAL OF NOVA SCOTIA
THE ATTORNEY GENERAL OF MANITOBA
THE ATTORNEY GENERAL OF BRITISH COLUMBIA
THE ATTORNEY GENERAL OF PRINCE EDWARD IS-
LAND
THE ATTORNEY GENERAL OF SASKATCHEWAN
THE ATTORNEY GENERAL OF ALBERTA
FOUR NATIONS CONFEDERACY INC.
(Intervenors)

118

AND IN THE MATTER of a Reference to the Court of Appeal of Quebec relative to a draft Resolution containing a joint address to Her Majesty The Queen concerning the Constitution of Canada

THE ATTORNEY GENERAL OF QUEBEC
          (Appellant/Respondent)

          —and—

THE ATTORNEY GENERAL OF CANADA
          (Respondent/Appellant)
     —and—

THE ATTORNEY GENERAL FOR MANITOBA
THE ATTORNEY GENERAL OF BRITISH COLUMBIA
THE ATTORNEY GENERAL OF PRINCE EDWARD ISLAND
THE ATTORNEY GENERAL OF ALBERTA
THE ATTORNEY GENERAL OF NOVA SCOTIA
THE ATTORNEY GENERAL OF SASKATCHEWAN
FOUR NATIONS CONFEDERACY INC.
     (Intervenors supporting the Attorney General of Quebec)

          —and—

THE ATTORNEY GENERAL OF ONTARIO
THE ATTORNEY GENERAL OF NEW BRUNSWICK
     (Intervenors supporting the Attorney General of Canada)

     CORAM:

     The Chief Justice and Martland, Ritchie, Dickson, Beetz, Estey, McIntyre, Chouinard and Lamer JJ.

     THE CHIEF JUSTICE AND ESTEY AND McINTYRE JJ.

     These reasons are addressed solely to Question 2 in the Manitoba and Newfoundland References and the conventional segment of Question B in the Quebec Reference. Our views upon the other questions raised in the three References are expressed in another judgment. As will be pointed out later, no legal question is raised in the questions under consideration in these reasons and, ordinarily, the Court would not undertake to answer them for it is not the function of the Court to go beyond legal determinations. Because of the unusual nature of these References and because the issues raised in the questions now before us were argued at some length before the Court and have become the subject of the reasons of the majority, with which, with the utmost deference, we cannot agree, we feel obliged to answer the questions notwithstanding their extra-legal nature.

Question 2 in the Manitoba and Newfoundland References is in the form set out hereunder:

2. Is it a constitutional convention that the House of Commons and Senate of Canada will not request Her Majesty the Queen to lay before the Parliament of the United Kingdom of Great Britain and Northern Ireland a measure to amend the Constitution of Canada affecting federal-provincial relationships or the powers, rights or privileges granted or secured by the Constitution of Canada to the provinces, their legislatures or governments without first obtaining the agreement of the provinces?

The same question arises from the wording of Question B in the Quebec Reference which asks: (Translation)

B. Does the Canadian Constitution empower, whether by statute, convention or otherwise, the Senate and the House of Commons of Canada to cause the Canadian Constitution to be amended without the consent off the provinces and in spite of the objection of several of them, in such a manner as to affect:

(i) the legislative competence of the provincial legislatures in virtue of the Canadian Constitition?

(ii) the status or role of the provincial legislatures or governments within the Canadian Federation?

At the outset it should be observed that the convention referred to in the above questions, and contended for by all objecting provinces except Saskatchewan, is a constitutional convention which requires that before the two Houses of the Canadian Parliament will request Her Majesty the Queen to lay before the Parliament of the United Kingdom a measure to amend the Constitution of Canada, affecting federal-provincial relations, it will obtain agreement thereto from the Provinces. From the wording of the questions and from the course of argument it is clear that the questions mean the consent of all the Provinces. This then is the question which must be answered on this part of the References. An affirmative answer would involve a declaration that such a convention, requiring the consent of all the Provinces, exists, while a negative answer would, of course, deny its existence. No other answers can be open to the Court for, on a reference of this nature, the Court may answer only the questions put and may not conjure up questions of its own which, in turn, would lead to uninvited answers: see *Reference re Magistrates' Courts of Quebec*, (1965) S.C.R. 772 (pp. 779-780); *Lord's Day Alliance of Canada v. Attorney-General for Manitoba*, (1925) A.C. 384; *Attorney-General For The Province of Ontario v. Attorney-General For The Dominion of Canada and Another*, (1912) A.C. 571; and *Reference re Waters and Water-Powers*, (1929) S.C.R. 200.

The position was expressed succinctly in the *Lord's Day Alliance* case by Lord Blanesburgh, at pp. 388-389. He said:

It will be observed that each of these questions is concerned with a state of things resulting from the new Act being duly brought into force. The Lieutenant-Governor-in-Council expresses a desire to be informed as to the legality of the excursions to which he refers only on the assumption that the Act has been made operative, and no question as to their legality apart from the Act has been made operative, and no question as to their legality apart from the Act is propounded. Their Lordships were, however, strongly urged by the appellants to deal with and dispose of the view that such excursions were lawful in Manitoba independently of the Act altogether — a view expressed by some of the learned judges of the Court of Appeal in this case and foreshadowed in an earlier decision of the same Court.

Their Lordships will refrain from taking this course, for one compelling reason, which they name out of several which would justify reserve in this matter.

Statutes empowering the executive Government, whether of the Dominion of Canada or of a Canadian Province, to obtain by direct request from the Court answers to questions both of fact and law, although intra vires of the respective Legislatures, impose a novel duty to be discharged, but not enlarged by the Court: see *Attorney-General for Ontario v. Attorney-General for Canada* (1912 A.C. 571) It is more than ordinarily expedient in the case of such references that a Court should refrain from dealing with questions other than those which on excessive responsibility are in express terms referred to it, and their Lordships will here act upon that view.

Where there is ambiguity, or where questions are phrased in such general terms that a precise answer is difficult or impossible to give, the Court may qualify the answers, answer in general terms, or refuse to answer: see *Reference re Waters and Water-Powers, supra.* No such considerations apply here. There is no ambiguity in the questions before the Court. Question 2 in the Manitoba and Newfoundland References refers without qualification to the "agreement of the provinces." Question B in the Quebec Referene uses the words "the consent of the provinces," also without qualification. The expressions "of the provinces" or "of the provinces of Canada" in this context and in general usage mean in plain English *all* of the Provinces of Canada, and our consideration of the questions must be upon this basis. The Court, in our view, would not be justified in editing the questions to develop a meaning not clearly expressed. These expressions in ordinary usage mean each of the Provinces. This, in turn, connotes all of the provinces. This is so because the question assumes that all provinces are equal regarding their respective constitutional positions. Where the expression "Houses of Parliament" is used in many instances in the record before this Court on these appeals it could hardly be argued that the expression could mean either or one of the Houses of Parliament; that is to say, if the consent of the Houses of Parliament were required by statue, the provision could not be read as including the possibility that the consent of one of the Houses of Parliament would be sufficient. So it is with the questions before us

What are conventions and, particularly, what are constitutional conventions? While our answer to Question 2 in the Manitoba and Newfoundland References and the conventional segment of Question B in the Quebec Reference will differ from those of the majority of the Court, we are in agreement with much of what has been said as to the general nature of constitutional conventions in the reasons for judgment by the majority, which we have had the advantage of reading. We are in agreement, as well, with the words of Freedman C.J.M. in his reasons for judgment in the Manitoba Reference, referred to with approval and quoted by the majority. We cannot, however, agree with any suggestion that the non-observance of a convention can properly be termed unconstitutional in any strict or legal sense, or that its observance could be, in any sense, a constitutional requirement within the meaning of Question 3 of the Manitoba and Newfoundland References. In a federal state where the essential feature of the Constitution must be the distribution of powers between the two levels of government, each supreme in its own legislative sphere, constitutionality and legality must be synonymous, and conventional rules will be accorded less significance than they may have in a unitary state such as the United Kingdom. At the risk of undue repetition, the point must again be made that constitutionalism in a unitary state and practices in the national and regional political units of a federal state must be differentiated from constitutional law in a federal state. Such law cannot be ascribed to informal or customary origins, but mut be found in a formal document which is the source of authority, legal authority, through which the central and regional units function and exercise their powers.

The Constitution of Canada, as has been pointed out by the majority, is only in part written, i.e. contained in statues which have the force of law and which include, in addition to the *British North America Act* (hereinafter called the *BNA Act*), the various other enactments which are listed in the reasons of the majority. Another, and indeed highly important, part of the Constitution has taken the form of custom and usage, adopting in large part the practices of the Parliament of the United Kingdom and adapting them to the federal nature of this country. These have evolved with time to form with the statues referred to above and certain rules of the common law a Constitution for Canada. This Constitution depends then on statutes and common law rules which declare the law and have the force of law, and upon customs, usages and conventions developed in political science which, while not having the force of law in the sense that there is a legal enforcement process or sanction available for their breach, form a vital part of the Constitution without which it would be incomplete and unable to serve its purpose.

As has been pointed out by the majority, a fundamental difference between the legal, that is the statutory and common law rules of the Constitution, and the conventional rules is that, while a breach of the legal rules, whether of statutory or common law nature, has a legal consequence in that it will be restrained by the courts, no such sanction exists for breach or non-observance of the conventional rules. The observance of constitutional conventions depends upon the acceptance of the obligation of conformance by the actors deemed to be bound thereby. When this consideration is insufficient to compel observance no court may enforce the convention by legal action. The sanction for non-observance of a convention is political in that disregard of a convention may lead to political defeat, to loss of office, or to other political consequences, but it will not engage the attention of the courts which are limited to matters of law alone. Courts, however, may recognize the existence of conventions and that is what is asked of us in answering the questions. The answer, whether affirmative or negative however, can have no legal effect, and acts performed or done in conformance with the law, even though in direct contradiction of well-established conventions, will not be enjoined or set aside by the courts. For one of many examples of the application of this principle see: *Stella Madzimbamuto v. Desmond William Lardner-Burke and Frederick Phillip George*, (1969) 1 A.C. 645. Simple convention cannot create such a power in either level of government. A Canadian convention could only be of negative effect, that is, to limit the exercise of such power where it exists in law.

There are different kinds of conventions and usages, but we are concerned here with what may be termed "constitutional" conventions or rules of the Constitution. They were described by Professor Dicey in the tenth edition of his *Law Of The Constitution*, at pp. 23-24, in the following passage:

The one set of rules are in the strictest sense "laws," since they are rules which (whether written or unwritten, whether enacted by statute or derived from the mass of custom, tradition, or judge-made maxims known as the common law) are enforced by the courts; these rules constitute "constitutional law" in the proper sense of that term, and may for the sake of distinction be called collectively "the law of the constitution."

The other set of rules consist of conventions, understandings, habits, or practices which, though they may regulate the conduct of the several members of the sovereign power, of the Ministry, or of other officials, are not in reality laws at all since they are not enforced by the courts. This portion of constitutional law may, for the sake of distinction, be termed the "conventions of the constitution," or constitutional morality.

Later, at page 27, after discussing examples from English practice, he said:

Under the English constitution they have one point in common: they are none of them "laws" in the true sense of the word, for if any or all of them were broken, no court would take notice of their violation.

And further, at pp. 30-31, he added:

With conventions or understandings he (the lawyer and law teacher) has no direct concern. They vary from generation to generation, almost from year to year. Whether a Ministry defeated at the polling booths ought to retire on the day when the result of the election is known, or may more properly retain office until after a defeat in Parliament, is or may be a question of practical importance. The opinions on this point which prevail today differ (it is said) from the opinions or understandings which prevailed thirty years back, and are possibly different from the opinions or understandings which may prevail ten years hence. Weighty precedents and high authority are cited on either side of this knotty question; the dicta or practice of Russell and Peel may be balanced off against the dicta or practice of Beaconsfield and Gladstone. The subject, however, is not one of law but of politics, and need trouble no lawyer or the class of any professor of law. If he is concerned with it at all, he is so only in so far as he may be called upon to show what is the connection (if any there be) between the conventions of the constitution and the law of the constitution.

This view has been adopted by Canadian writers, *e.g.* Professor Peter K. Hogg in *Constitutional Law of Canada* dealt with the matter in these terms, at page 7:

Conventions are rules of the constitution which are not enforced by the law courts. Because they are not enforced by the law courts they are best regarded as non-legal rules, but because they do in fact regulate the working of the constitution they are an important concern of the constitutional lawyer. What conventions do is to prescribe the way in which legal powers shall be exercised. Some conventions have the effect of transferring effective power from the legal hold to another official or institution. Other conventions limit an apparently broad legal power, or even prescribe that a legal power shall not be exercised at all.

At page 8, he said:

If a convention is disobeyed by an official, then it is common, especially in the United Kingdom, to describe the official's act or omission as "unconstitutional". But this use of the term unconstitutional must be carefully distinguished from the case where a legal rule of the constitution has been disobeyed. Where unconstitutionality springs from a breach of law, the purported act is normally a nullity and there is a remedy available in the courts. But where "unconstitutionality" springs merely from a breach of convention, no breach of the law has occurred and no legal remedy will be available. If a court did give a remedy for a breach of convention, for example, by declaring invalid a statute enacted for Canada by the United Kingdom Parliament without Canada's request or consent, or by ordering an unwilling Governor General to give his assent to a bill enacted by both houses of Parliament, then we should have to change our language and describe the rule which used to be thought of as a convention as a rule of the common law. In other words a judicial decision could have the effect of transforming a conventional rule into a legal rule. A convention may also be transformed into law by being enacted as a statute.

It will be noted that Professor Hogg, in the quotation immediately above, has expressed the view that a judicial

125

decision could have the effect of transforming a conventional rule into a legal rule, as could the enactment of a convention in statutory form. There can be no doubt that a statute, by enacting the terms of a convention, could create positive law, but it is our view that it is not for the Courts to raise a convention to the status of a legal principle. As pointed out above, courts may recognize the existence of conventions in their proper sphere. That is all that may be properly sought from the Court in answering Question 2 in the Manitoba and Newfoundland References and the conventional part of Question B in the Quebec Reference: an answer by the Court recognizing the existence of the convention or denying its existence. For the Court to postulate some other convention requiring less than unanimous provincial consent to constitutional amendments would be to go beyond the terms of the References and in so doing to answer a question not posed in the References. It would amount, in effect, to an attempt by judicial pronouncement to create an amending formula for the Canadian Constitution which, in addition to being beyond the Court's power to declare, not being raised in a question posed in any of the References before the Court, would be incomplete for failure to specify the degree or percentage of provincial consent required. Furthermore, all the Provinces, with the exception of Saskatchewan, oppose such a step. Those favouring the position of the federal Parliament, Ontario and New Brunswick, do so because they say no convention exists and those attacking the federal position, Quebec, Nova Scotia, Prince Edward Island, Manitoba, Alberta and British Columbia, do so because they say provincial participation is already fixed by what may be called "the rule of unanimity."

Conventions, while frequently unwritten, may nonetheless be reduced to writing. They may be reached by specific agreement between the parties to be bound, or they may more commonly arise from practice and usage. It is true, as well, that conventions can become law but this, in our view, would require some formal legal step such as enactment in statutory form. *The Statute of Westminster* of 1931 affords an example of the enactment of conventions concerning constitutional relations between the United King-

126

dom and the various Dominions. However a convention may arise or be created, the essential condition for its recognition must be that the parties concerned regard it as binding upon them. While a convention, by its very nature, will often lack the precision and clearness of expression of a law, it must be recognized, known and understood with sufficient clarity that conformance is possible and a breach of conformance immediately discernible, It must play as well a necessary constitutional role.

There are many such conventions of the Canadian Constitution and while at different periods they may have taken different forms, and while change and development have been observable and are, no doubt, continuing processes, they have been recognized nonetheless as rules or conventions of the Canadian Constitution, known and observed at any given time in Canadian affairs. As the reasons of the majority point out, there are many examples. The general rule that the Governor General will act only according to the advice of the Prime Minister is purely conventional and is not to be found in any legal enactment. In the same category is the rule that after a general election the Governor General will call upon the leader of the party with the greatest number of seats to form a government. The rule of responsible government that a government losing the confidence of the House of Commons must itself resign, or obtain a dissolution, the general principles of majority rule and responsible government underlying the daily workings of the institutions of the executive and legislative branches of each level of government, and a variety of other such conventional arrangements, serve as further illustrations. These rules have an historical origin and bind, and have bound, the actors in constitutional matters in Canada for generations. No one can doubt their operative force or the reality of their existence as an effective part of the Canadian Constitution. They are, nonetheless, conventional and, therefore, distinct from purely legal rules. They are observed without demur because all parties concerned recognize their existence and accept the obligation of observance, considering themselves to be bound. Even though it may be, as the majority of the Court has said, a matter of some surprise to many Canadi-

127

ans, these conventions have no legal force. They are, in short, the product of political experience, the adoption of which allows the political process to function in a way acceptable to the community.

These then are recognized conventions, they are definite, understandable and understood. They have the unquestioned acceptance not only of the actors in political affairs but of the public at large. Can it be said that any convention having such clear definition and acceptance concerning provincial participation in the amendment of the Canadian Constitution has developed? It is in the light of this comparison that the existence of any supposed constitutional convention must be considered. It is abundantly clear, in our view, that the answer must be No. The degree of provincial participation in constitutional amendments has been a subject of lasting controversy in Canadian political life for generations. It cannot be asserted, in our opinion, that any view on this subject has become so clear and so broadly accepted as to constitute a constitutional convention. It should be observed that there is a fundamental difference between the convention in the Dicey concept and the convention for which some of the Provinces here contend. The Dicey convention relates to the functioning of individuals and institutions within a parliamentary democracy in unitary form. It does not qualify or limit the authority or sovereignty of Parliament or the Crown. The convention sought to be advanced here would truncate the functioning of the executive and legislative branches at the federal level. This would impose a limitation on the sovereign body itself within the Constitution. Surely such a convention would require for its recognition, even in the non-legal, political sphere, the clearest signal from the plenary unit intended to be bound, and not simply a plea from the majority of the beneficiaries of such a convention, the provincial plenary units.

An examination of the Canadian experience since Confederation will, bearing in mind the considerations above described, serve to support our conclusion on this question. It may be observed here that it was not suggested in argument before this Court that there was any procedure for amendment now available other than by the addresses of both Houses of Parliament to Her Majesty the Queen. It was argued, however, that this was a procedural step only and that before it could be undertaken by Parliament the consent of the Provinces would be required. It is with the frequency with which provincial consents were obtained or omitted, with the circumstances under which consent was or was not sought, with the nature of the amendments involved, and with provincial attitudes towards them that we must concern ourselves. As has been pointed out in other judgments on these References, here and in the other courts, there have been since Confederation some twenty-two amendments to the BNA Act. Brief particulars of each amendment taken from the Government paper entitled, "The Amendment of the Constitution of Canada", published in 1965 under the authority of the The Hon. Guy Favreau, the federal Minister of Justice, hereinafter referred to as the White Paper, are set out below for convenience of reference.

(1) The *Rupert's Land Act*, 1868 authorized the acceptance by Canada of the rights of the Hudson's Bay Company over Rupert's Land and the North-West Territory. It also provided that, on Address from the Houses of Parliament of Canada, the Crown could declare this territory part of Canada and the Parliament of Canada could make laws for its peace, order and good government.

(2) The *British North America Act of 1871* ratified the Manitoba Act passed by the Parliament of Canada in 1870, creating the province of Manitoba and giving it a province constitution similar to those of the other provinces. The British North America Act of 1871 also empowered the Parliament of Canada to establish new provinces out of any Canadian territory not then included in a province; to alter the boundaries of any province (with the consent of its legislature), and to provide for the administration, peace, order and good government of any territory not included in a province.

(3) The *Parliament of Canada Act of 1875* amended section 18 of the British North America Act, 1867, which set forth the privileges, immunities and powers of each of the Houses of Parliament.

(4) The *British North America Act of 1886* authorized the Parliament of Canada to provide for the representation in the Senate and the House of Commons of any territories not included in any province.

(5) The *Statute Law Revision Act*, 1893 repealed some obsolete provisions of the British North America Act of 1867.

(6) The *Canadian Speaker (Appointment of Deputy) Act*, 1895 confirmed and Act of the Parliament of Canada which provided for the appointment of a Deputy-Speaker for the Senate.

(7) The *British North America Act*, 1907 established a new scale of financial subsidies to the provinces in lieu of those set forth in section 118 of the British North America Act of 1867. While not expressly repealing the original section, it made its provisions obsolete.

(8) The *British North America Act*, 1915 redefined the Senatorial Divisions of Canada to take into account the provinces of Manitoba, British Columbia, Saskatchewan and Alberta. Although this statute did not expressly amend the text of the original section 22, it did alter its effect.

(9) The *British North America Act*, 1916 provided for the extension of the life of the current Parliament of Canada beyond the normal period of five years.

(10) The *Statute Law Revision Act*, 1927 repealed additional spent or obsolete provisions in the United Kingdom statutes, including two provisions of the British North America Acts.

(11) The *British North America Act*, 1930 confirmed the natural resources agreements between the Government of Canada and the Governments of Manitoba, British Columbia, Alberta and Saskatchewan, giving the agreements the force of law notwithstanding anything in the British North America Acts.

(12) The *Statute of Westminster*, 1931 while not directly amending the British North America Acts, did alter some of their provisions. Thus, the Parliament of Canada was given the power to make laws having extraterritorial effect. Also, Parliament and the provincial legislatures were given the authority, within their powers under the British North America Acts, to repeal any United Kingdom statute that formed part of the law of Canada. This authority, however, expressly excluded the British North America Act itself.

(13) The *British North America Act*, 1940 gave the Parliament of Canada the exclusive jurisdiction to make laws in relation to Unemployment Insurance.

(14) The *British North America Act*, 1943 provided for the postponement of redistribution of the seats in the House of Commons until the first session of Parliament after the cessation of hostilities.

(15) The *British North America Act*, 1946 replaced section 51 of the British North America Act, 1867, and altered the provisions for the readjustment of representation in the House of Commons.

(16) The *British North America Act*, 1949 confirmed the Terms of Union between Canada and Newfoundland.

(17) The *British North America Act*, (No. 2), 1949 gave the Parliament of Canada authority to amend the Constitution of Canada with certain exceptions.

(18) The *Statute Law Revision Act*, 1950 repealed an obsolete section of the British North America Act, 1867.

(19) The *British North America Act*, 1951 gave the Parliament of Canada concurrent jurisdiction with the provinces to make laws in relation to Old Age Pensions.

(20) The *British North America Act*, 1960 amended section 99 and altered the tenure of office of superior court judges.

(21) The *British North America Act*, 1964 amended the authority conferred upon the Parliament of Canada by the British North America Act, 1951, in relation to benefits supplementary to Old Age Pensions.

130

(22) *Amendment by Order in Council*

Section 146 of the British North America Act, 1867 provided for the admission of other British North American territories by Order in Council and stipulated that the provisions of any such Order in Council would have the same effect as if enacted by the Parliament of the United Kingdom. Under this section, Rupert's Land and the North-Western Territory were admitted by Order in Council on June 23rd, 1870; British Columbia by Order in Council on May 16th, 1871; Prince Edward Island by Order in Council on June 26th, 1873. Because all of these Orders in Council contained provisions of a constitutional character — adapting the provisions of the British North America Act to the new provinces, but with some modifications in each case — they may therefore be regarded as constitutional amendments.

In examining these amendments it must be borne in mind that all do not possess the same relevance or force for the purpose of this inquiry. Question 2 of the Manitoba and Newfoundland References and the conventional segment of Question B in the Quebec Reference raise the issue of the propriety of non-consensual amendments which affect federal-provincial relationships and the powers, rights and privileges of the Provinces. The questions do not limit consideration to those amendments which affected the distribution of legislative powers between the federal Parliament and the provincial legislatures. Since the distribution of powers is the very essence of a federal system, amendments affecting such distribution will be of especial concern to the Provinces. Precedents found in such amendments will be entitled to serious consideration. It does not follow, however, that other amendments which affected federal-provincial relationships without altering the distribution of powers should be disregarded in this inquiry. Consideration must be given in according weight to the various amendments, to the reaction they provoked from the Provinces. This is surely the real test of relevance in this discussion. On many occasions provinces considered that amendments not affecting the distribution of legislative power were sufficiently undesirable to call for strenuous opposition. The test of whether the convention exists, or has existed, is to be found by examining the results of such opposition. Professor William S. Livingston in *Federalism and Constitutional Change,* 1956 (Oxford University Press), made this comment, at page 62, when considering the 1943 amendment which did not affect the distribution of powers, and the 1940 amendment which did:

The important difference between the two amendments lies, of course, in the fact that that of 1940 clearly and significantly altered the distribution

131

of powers, a part of the constitution which, it has been argued, is especially deserving of the protection afforded by the principle of unanimous consent. But the facts themselves demonstrate that at least one of the provinces considered the alteration of 1943 sufficiently important to call for long and bitter protests at the disdainful attitude of the Dominion Government. If unanimity is for the protection of provinces, whether singly or collectively, it is reasonable to think that the provinces should be the ones to judge when it should be invoked. By the very operation of the principle, a province will not protest unless it considers the matter at hand worth protesting about.

The true test of the importance of the various amendments for our purpose is a consideration of the degree of provincial opposition they aroused, for whatever reason, the consideration that such opposition received, and the influence it had on the course of the amendment proceedings.

Prior to the amendment effected by the *BNA Act* of 1930 there were at least three amendments, those of 1886, 1907 and 1915, which substantially affected the Provinces and which were procured without the consent of all the Provinces. The amendment of 1886 gave power to Parliament to provide for parliamentary representation in the Senate and House of Commons for territories not forming part of any province, and therefore altered the provincial balance of representation. That of 1907 changed the basis of federal subsidies payable to the Provinces and thus directly affected the provincial interests. That of 1915 redefined territorial divisions for senatorial representation, and therefore had a potential for altering the provincial balance. Those of 1886 and 1915 were passed without provincial consultation or consent, and that of 1907 had the consent of all provinces save British Columbia, which actively opposed its passage both in Canada and in the United Kingdom. The amendment was passed with minor changes. These precedents, it may be said, should by themselves have only a modest influence in the consideration of the question before the Court. It is clear, however, that no support whatever for the convention may be found on an examination of the amendments made up to 1930. None had full provincial approval.

The *BNA Act* of 1930 provided for the transfer of natural resources within the provincial territories to the Provinces of Manitoba, Saskatchewan and Alberta. It also provided for the re-conveyance of certain railway lands to British Columbia. In effecting this amendment the consent of the Provinces directly concerned. *i.e.* the four western Provinces only, was obtained, although the arrangement had received the general approval of the other provinces as expressed at a conference in 1927. This is a precedent of modest weight, but it is worthy of note that despite the fact that the interests of all non-involved provinces were affected by the alienation of the assets formerly under federal control, it was not considered necessary to procure any formal consent from them. It is of more than passing interest to note that in the amending procedure provided for in the 1930 *British North America Act Amendment* there is no requirement for consent or participation by any of the other five provinces (as they then were) although their indirect interest in federal resources might be affected.

The amendments of 1943, 1946, 1949, 1949(2), 1950 and 1960 were not considered of great significance on this issue by the parties and little comment was made upon them but all, save that of 1960, were achieved without full provincial consent. This, subject to what is later said concerning the 1943 amendment, leaves for consideration the *Statute of Westminster* of 1931 and the amendments of 1940, 1951 and 1964. The *Statute of Westminster* and the amendments of 1940, 1951 and 1964 affected the Provinces directly. Canadian participation in the settlement of the provisions of the Statute and the said amendments had the consent of all provinces. These examples were heavily relied upon by the objecting provinces to support an affirmative answer to Question 2 of the Manitoba and Newfoundland References and the negative answer to the conventional part of Question B of the Quebec Reference. As to the *Statute of Westminster*, it freed federal and provincial legislation from the restrictions imposed by the *Colonial Laws Validity Act* of 1865 and gave statutory recognition to certain conventions which had grown up with the development of self-government in the former colonies. The pre-existing division of legislative power between federal and provincial legislatures in Canada was not, however, in any way affected and it did not recognize or give statutory form to any convention requiring provincial consent to the amendment of the *BNA Act*.

In fact, it specifically excepted the question of *BNA Act* amendments from its purview in s. 7, ss. 1.

The amendment of 1940 transferring legislative power over unemployment insurance to the federal Parliament also had full provincial consent. It must be observed there, however, that when questioned in the House of Commons on this point Mr. Mackenzie King, then Prime Minister, while acknowledging that consents had been obtained, specifically stated that this course had been followed to avoid any constitutional issue on this point and he disclaimed any necessity for such consent. The following interchange is recorded in the House of Commons Debates, 1940, pp. 1117 and 1122:

> *Mr. Mackenzie King:* . . . We have avoided anything in the nature of coercion of any of the provinces. Moreover we have avoided the raising of a very critical constitutional question, namely, whether or not in amending the British North America Act it is absolutely necessary to secure the consent of all the provinces, or whether the consent of a certain number of provinces would of itself be sufficient. That question may come up but not in reference to unemployment insurance at some time later on.
>
> . . . . . .
>
> *Mr. J. T. Thorson (Selkirk):* I shall be only a few moments in my advocacy of this resolution. Unemployment insurance is a very important part of the programme of national reform upon which this country must embark. I wish, however, to dispute the contention that it is necessary to obtain the consent of the provinces before an application is made to amend the British North America Act. In my opinion there is no such necessity. On the other hand, it is the course of wisdom to advance as advances may be properly made, and I am sure that every hon. member is very glad that all the provinces of Canada have agreed to this measure. But I would not wish this debate to conclude with an acceptance, either direct or implied, of the doctrine that it is necessary to obtain the consent of the provinces before an application is made to amend the British North America Act. Fortunately, this is an academic question at this time.
>
> *Mr. Lapointe (Quebec East):* May I tell my hon. friend that neither the Prime Minister nor I have said it is necessary but it may be desirable.
>
> *Mr. Thorson:* The Prime Minister (Mr. Mackenzie King) has made it perfectly clear that the question does not enter into this discussion, in view of the fact that all the provinces have signified their willingness that this amendment should be requested.

It appears from the foregoing that the then Prime Minister recognized the existence of a question on this point. It cannot be said, however, that his words support the view that he considered that there was any convention requiring provincial consent in existence. It is clear, we suggest, that he procured the consent of the provinces on that occasion in order to avoid raising any question on the subject and as a measure of good politics rather than as a constitutional requirement. It is surely obvious that the federal government would always prefer to have, as a political matter, provincial approval, but the position of the federal authorities as expressed in the foregoing Parliamentary exchange does not support the proposition that they considered that they were bound any convention.

We are aware, of course, that other declarations have been made upon this subject by persons of high political rank as well as academics of high standing.

Many such pronouncements were cited in argument before us. We do not propose to deal with them in detail. It is sufficient to say that many favour the existence of the convention; many deny its existence. Some of the authors of such statements have contradicted themselves on the point at different times in their careers. The debate on this question has been active and long drawn out but, in our view, has never been resolved in favour of the existence of the convention. The continuation of controversy on the subject among political and academic figures only adds additional weight to the contention that no convention of provincial consent has achieved constitutional recognition to this day.

The amendment of 1951 had full approval from the Provinces, as did that of 1964. The 1951 amendment gave power relating to old age pensions to the federal Parliament and the 1964 amendment was merely a supplementary tidying-up of the original 1951 provisions. In our view, they dealt with the same matter and can stand as only one precedent favouring the existence of the convention.

After examining the amendments made since Confederation, and after observing that out of the twenty-two amendments listed above only in the case of four was unanimous provincial consent sought or obtained and, even after according special weight to those amendments relied on by the Provinces, we cannot agree that history justifies a conclusion that the convention contended for by the Provinces has emerged.

Great weight was put upon the 1940 *Unemployment Insurance Act* amendment as a precedent favouring the existence of the convention. Despite the obtaining of provincial consent for the 1940 amendment, the federal government proceeded three years later to the completion of the amendment of 1943 without provincial consent and in the face of the strong protests of the Province of Quebec. This amendment did not touch provincial powers. It dealt with the postponement of redistribution of seats in the House of Commons. Nevertheless, it was deemed off sufficient importance by Quebec because its interest was particularly affected to arouse active opposition which was overborne by the federal government in procuring the amendment. Livingston, in discussing this amendment in his text, referred to above, said, at p. 61:

But though the treatment of the 1940 Act came dangerously near acceptance of the principle of unanimous consent, the procedure followed in 1943 destroyed all hope that the question had been settled. The 1943 amendment was for the purpose of postponing the redistribution of seats in the House of Commons until after the war. The redistribution was prescribed by the constitution (Sec. 51) and it therefore required an Act of the British Parliament to postpone it. Quebec, whose population had increased more than that of other provinces, was to benefit considerably from the reassignment of seats and was loath to postpone it. But the inconvenience and injustice of reorganizing the basis of representation in wartime impelled the Government to push its proposal through the House.

It was introduced and defended by Mr. St. Laurent, then Minister of Justice, and was supported by both Opposition parties; the issue in the House was never in serious doubt. There was no effort on the part of the Dominion Government to consult the provinces, and this action evoked no protest except on the part of Quebec. This province, however, objected strongly to the Government's treatment of the matter and protests were voiced both at Quebec and at Ottawa. The provincial legislature passed a resolution of protest which the Government was requested to transmit to the British Government. Mackenzie King refused, however, replying that the matter concerned only the Dominion Parliament and not the provincial legislatures; that the compact theory was indefensible both in theory and in law; and that the British could not take cognizance of such a communication, since it was bound by the address of the Dominion Parliament. In the House bitter complaints were heard that the Government was simply ignoring the official protest of the Quebec legislature and that such high-handedness abused the constitution and violated the rights of the provinces. But the Government, secure in the support of the Opposition, pressed the matter to a vote without even replying to these protestations.

In summary, we observe that in the one hundred and fourteen years since confederation Canada has grown from a group of four somewhat hesitant colonies into a modern, independent state, vastly increased in size, power and wealth, and having a social and governmental structure unimagined in 1867. It cannot be denied that vast change has occurred in Dominion-Provincial relations over that period. Many factors have influenced this process and the amendments to the BNA Act — all the amendments — have played a significant part and all must receive consideration in resolving this question. Only in four cases has full provincial consent been obtained and in many cases the federal government has proceeded with amendments in the face of active provincial opposition. In our view, it is unrealistic in the extreme to say that the convention has emerged.

As a further support for the convention argument, the White Paper referred to above was cited and relied upon. It was asserted that the statement of principles set out, at page 15, being an authoritative government pronouncement, was decisive on the point. The summary of principles is set out hereunder:

The first general principle that emerges in the foregoing resume is that although the enactment by the United Kingdom is necessary to amend the British North America Act, such action is taken only upon formal request from Canada. No Act of the United Kingdom Parliament affecting Canada is therefore passed unless it is requested and consented to by Canada. Conversely, every amendment requested by Canada in the past has been enacted.

The second general principle is that the sanction of Parliament is required for a request to the British Parliament for an amendment to the British North America Act. This principle was established early in the history of Canada's constitutional amendments, and has not been violated since 1895. The procedure invariably is to seek amendments by a joint Address of the Canadian House of Commons and Senate to the Crown.

The third general principle is that no amendment to Canada's Constitution will be made by the British Parliament merely upon the request of a Canadian province. A number of attempts to secure such amendments have been made, but none has been successful. The first such attempt was made as early as 1868, by a province which was at that time dissatisfied with the terms of Confederation. This was followed by other attempts in 1869, 1874 and 1887. The British Government refused in all cases to act on provincial government representations on the grounds that it should not intervene in the affairs of Canada except at the request of the federal government representing all of Canada.

The fourth general principle is that the Canadian Parliament will not request an amendment directly affecting federal-provincial relationships without prior consultation and agreement with the provinces. This principle did not emerge as early as others but since 1907, and particularly since 1930, has gained increasing recognition and acceptance. The nature and the degree of provincial participation in the amending process, however, have not lent themselves to easy definition.

It is the fourth principle which is stressed by the objecting provinces. In our view, they have attributed too much significance to this statement of the four principles. The author of the White Paper was at pains to say, at page 11:

Certain rules and principles relating to amending procedures have nevertheless developed over the years. They have emerged from the practices and procedures employed in securing various amendments to the British

137

North America Act since 1867. *Though not constitutionally binding in any strict sense, they have come to be recognized and accepted in practice as part of the amendment process in Canada.* (emphasis added).

It would not appear that he was satisfied that the principles had become so well-established that they had acquired strict constitutional force. Furthermore, we are unable to accord to the fourth principle the significance given to it by the objecting provinces. The first sentence pronounces strongly in favour of the existence of the convention. If it stopped there, subject to what the author had said earlier, it would constitute a statement of great weight. However, the third sentence contradicts the first and, in fact, cancels it out. By suggesting the possibility of a requirement of partial provincial consent it answers Question 2 in the Manitoba and Newfoundland Refereces and the conventional segment of Question B in the Quebec Reference against the Provinces. "Increasing recognition", that is 'partial' but not 'complete' recognition, is all that is claimed by the author of the White Paper. A convention requires universal recognition by the actors in a scheme and this is certainly so where, as here, acceptance of a convention involves the surrender of a power by a sovereign body said to be a party to the convention. Furthermore, in recognizing uncertainty in specifying the degree of provincial participation, it denies the existence of any convention including that suggested by the Province of Saskatchewan. If there is difficulty in defining the degree of provincial participation, which there surely is, it cannot be said that any convention on the subject has been settled and recognized as a constitutional condition for the making of an amendment. It is the very difficulty of fixing the degree of provincial participation which, while it remains unresolved, prevents the formation or recognition of any convention. It robs any supposed convention of that degree of definition which is necessary to allow for its operation, for its binding effect upon the persons deemed to be bound, and it renders difficult if not impossible any clear discernment of a breach of the convention. In our view, then the fourth principle enunciated in the White Paper does not advance the provincial argument.

It was also argued that Canada was formed as a federal union and that the existence of a legal power of the central government to unilaterally change the Constitution was inimical to the concept of federalism. The convention then, it was argued, arose out of the necessity to restrain such unilateral conduct and preserve the federal nature of Canada. In this connection, it must be acknowledged at once that, in a federal union, the powers and rights of each of the two levels of government must be protected from the assault of the other. The whole history of constitutional litigation in Canada since Confederation has been concerned with this vital question. We are asked to say whether the need for the preservation of the principles of Canadian federalism dictates the necessity for a convention, requiring consent from the Provinces as a condition of the exercise by the federal government of its legal powers, to procure amendment to the Canadian Constitution. If the convention requires only partial consent, as is contended by Saskatchewan, it is difficult to see how the federal concept is thereby protected for, while those provinces favouring amendment would be pleased, those refusing consent could claim coercion.

If unanimous consent is required (as contended by the other objecting provinces), while it may be said that in general terms the concept of federalism would be protected it would only be by overlooking the special nature of Canadian federalism that this protection would be achieved. The *BNA Act* has not created a perfect or ideal federal state. Its provisions have accorded a measure of paramountcy to the federal Parliament. Certainly this has been done in a more marked degree in Canada than in many other federal states. For example, one need only look to the power of reservation and disallowance of provincial enactments; the power to declare works in a province to be for the benefit of all Canada and to place them under federal regulatory control; the wide powers to legislate generally for the peace, order and good government of Canada as a whole; the power to enact the criminal law of the entire country; the power to create and admit provinces out of existing territories and, as well, the paramountcy accorded federal legislation. It is this special nature of Canadian federalism which deprives the federalism argument described above of its force. This is particularly true when it involves the final settlement of Canadian constitutional affairs with an external government, the federal authority being the sole conduit for communication between Canada and the Sovereign and Canada alone having the power to deal in external matters. We therefore reject the argument that the preservation of the principles of Canadian federalism requires the recognition of the convention asserted before us.

While it may not be necessary to do so in dealing with Question 2, we feel obliged to make a further comment related to the federalism argument. It was argued that the federal authorities were assuming a power to act without restraint in disregard of provincial wishes which could go so far as to convert Canada into a unitary state by means of a majority vote in the House of Parliament. A few words will suffice to lay that argument at rest. What is before the Court is the task of answering the questions posed in three references. As has been pointed out, the Court can do no more than that. The questions all deal with the constitutional validity of precise proposals for constitutional amendment and they form the complete subject-matter of the Court's inquiry and our comments must be made with reference to them.

It is not for the Court to express views on the wisdom or lack of wisdom of these proposals. We are concerned solely with their constitutionality. In view of the fact that the unitary argument has been raised, however, it should be noted, in our view, that the federal constitutional proposals, which preserve a federal state without disturbing the distribution or balance of power, would create an amending formula which would enshrine provincial rights on the question of amendments on a secure, legal and constitutional footing, and would extinguish, as well, any presently existing power on the part of the federal Parliament to act unilaterally in constitutional matters. In so doing, it may be said that the Parliamentary resolution here under examination does not, save for the enactment of the *Charter of Rights*, which circumscribes the legislative powers of both the federal and provincial Legislatures, truly amend the Canadian Constitution. Its effect is to complete the formation of an incomplete constitution by supplying its present deficiency, i.e. an amending formula, which will enable the Constitution to be amended in Canada as befits a sovereign state. We are not here faced with an action which in any way has the effect of transforming this federal union into a unitary state. The *in terrorem* argument raising the spectre of a unitary state has no validity.

For the above reasons we answer the questions posed in the three References as follows:

Manitoba and Newfoundland References
Question 2: No

Quebec Reference
Question B (i) Yes
(ii) Yes

Other Books on Canadian Politics and History

CANADA'S OIL MONOPOLY
The Story of the $12 Billion Rip-off of Canadian Consumers

Highlights from the 1600-page study of Canada's oil industry prepared after an eight-year investigation by officials of Consumer and Corporate Affairs. The study led to public hearings by the Restrictive Trade Practices Commission. This abridgement was independently prepared by James Lorimer. Available in paperback only.

ISBN 0-88862-514-6 (paper)

REGIONAL DISPARITIES
Paul Phillips

The first comprehensive treatment of the regional disparities problem, this book examines Canadian regional economies, discusses strengths and weaknesses, and reviews the reasons for failure in national policies aimed at unifying the country. A book in the *Economy in Crisis* series.

ISBN 0-88862-206-6 (paper)   0-88862-207-4 (cloth)

HOW OTTAWA DECIDES
Planning and Industrial Policy-Making 1968-80

Richard D. French

A decisive study of the people who wield power in the federal government and of their continuing failure to coordinate and rationalize policy-making. Federal policies regarding industrial development and a national industrial strategy are examined in detail. A book in the *Canadian Institute for Economic Policy* series.

ISBN 0-88862-368-2 (paper)   0-88862-369-0 (cloth)

WHAT DOES QUEBEC WANT?
André Bernard

Written specifically for English Canadians by prominent Quebec political scientist André Bernard, this book provides an authoritative and impartial description of what most French-speaking Quebeckers agree on and where their main differences arise regarding the future of Quebec and Canada.

ISBN 0-88862-191-4 (paper)   0-88862-190-6 (cloth)

THE ASBESTOS STRIKE
Edited by Pierre Elliott Trudeau
Translated by James Boake

A classic in the literature of Canadian labour relations. The Asbestos strike brought into public prominence Pierre Elliott Trudeau, who worked on the side of the strikers in a confrontation which pitted workers against both company and government. Trudeau later brought together contributors to write this exhaustive analysis of a key event in Quebec's post-war history.

ISBN 0-88862-055-1 (paper)

POISONS IN PUBLIC
Case Studies of Environmental Pollution in Canada
Ross Howard

Author and journalist Ross Howard explores four representative instances of pollution affecting the lives of Canadians to illustrate why these problems persist and why they are often not cleaned up after citizen protest. Particular attention is paid to the workings of the political process and the role of government in responding to pressures from business and environmental groups. A book in the *Citizens and the Environment* series.

ISBN 0-88862-300-3 (paper)   0-88862-301-1 (cloth)